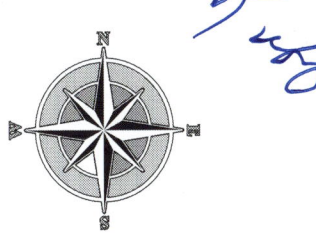

LETTERS TO MY CHILDREN

An autobiography by
FRANK A. RUFFO JR.

TO THE LOVES OF MY LIFE
Sandy, Brian, and Tina

FRANK ARTHUR RUFFO, JR.
Born June 6, 1942

CONTENTS

MY LIFE PRINCIPLES 1
PROLOGUE 5

LETTER ONE: TO MY CHILDREN 9
    Early Years (1942-1956) 11
    High School (1956-1960) 17
    College (1960-1964) 22
    Navy (1965-1968) 24
    Marriage and Divorce, etc.(1968-1985) 25
    Second Marriage (1985-Present) 30
    Philosophy and Conclusions 33

LETTER TWO: TO MY CHILDREN 43
    School Years (1947-1964) 45
    Navy (1965-1968) 48
    Civilian Life (1968-Present) 52
    Environmentalism 65
    Global Warming and Climate Change 72
    Entitlement Programs 76
    Abortion 79
    Civil Rights 82
    Gay and Lesbian Rights 85
    The Media 87
    Philosophy on American Government 90

LETTER THREE: TO MY CHILDREN 97
    Early Years (1942-1956) 99
    Preschool 99
    Grade School 101
    Junior High School 104
    The Beach 105
    High School (1956-1960) 109
    College (1960-1964) 119
    Christmas Break (1964) 130

Navy (1965-1968) 133
Civilian Life to Retirement 162
    1968-1976 162
    1976-1989 170
    1990-1993 200
    1994-1999 209
    2000-2007 221
    2008 to Present 228

EPILOGUE 233

PEARLS AND PREDICTIONS 237
    Pearls 239
    Predictions 241
    My Best Friends 244

MY CHALLENGES AND FRUSTRATIONS 249

Photo Gallery 253
Acknowledgements 269
Bibliography 271

"The greatest orator, save one, of antiquity, has left it on record that he always studied his adversary's case with as great, if not still greater, intensity than even his own. What Cicero practiced as the means of forensic success requires to be imitated by all who study any subject in order to arrive at the truth. He who knows only his own side of the case knows little of that. His reasons may be good, and no one may have been able to refute them. But if he is equally unable to refute the reasons on the opposite side, if he does not so much as know what they are, he has no ground for preferring either opinion. The rational position for him would be suspension of judgment."

John Stuart Mill

FRANK A. RUFFO JR.

LETTERS TO MY CHILDREN

FRANK A. RUFFO JR.

MY LIFE PRINCIPLES

FRANK A. RUFFO JR.

Because the universe is so vast, so old and so complicated, it seems reasonable to assume that there had to be a Designer. This cannot be said with absolute certainty; therefore all else is based on faith. A person is free to practice or not practice any faith that does not harm individuals or society. Organized religions have good and bad aspects, but none is essential for participation in any after-life if such exists.

To achieve happiness requires individual freedom. Government is necessary to protect the individual freedoms of its countrymen. If allowed to govern without control, it will develop into a monster that will ultimately destroy the society it was created to protect.

Government needs to be as small as possible to meet its charge and power kept at the lowest level possible. Government welfare systems are not good for a productive society except in cases of demonstrated inability for individuals to provide for themselves and offered only so long as they cannot or will not provide for themselves. Individual effort is the key to society's success. Both success and failure are expected and government needs to enter this arena with great caution and only if it is absolutely necessary to preserve our capitalistic system. Otherwise, it is "hands off" no matter what the short term effects may be.

Family is the key to individual and societal well-being. Family is comprised of a married man and woman and, if they so choose, as many children as they desire and can support. Individuals who may chose to remain single can make a valuable contribution to themselves and society. Good health, a loving family and close friends are the key to happiness and require considerable individual effort to achieve.

Racial prejudice will create havoc in a society, but providing preferences, laws or privileges, to attempt to right past injustices only adds fuel to division and will increase chaos.

We must be long term stewards for the protection of our environment and develop truly sustainable resources for our survival.

We must shift our focus to long term strategies for sources of energy rather than focus on short term fads like the "Green Movement", or a perceived energy shortage based on price/demand fluctuations or natural occurrences such as global warming and cooling, and extinction of species since there always has and always will be species extinction (eventually including Homo Sapiens).

LETTERS TO MY CHILDREN

PROLOGUE

FRANK A. RUFFO JR.

This book is written for you, my children, to memorialize for you what truths I believe I have gained, theories that, I believe, are close to truth; beliefs that have some credibility, as well as those that don't, and those views that are, at best, myths, and at worst, outright fantasy or lies. These conclusions are based on a combination of my own life experiences, absorbing the thoughts of others through many discussions and readings, from authors both dead and alive, and through critical reflection of what is real from what is not or may not be real.

These writings are for you so you might glean something from your father's life experience. Although I have a formal education, as you know, I do not have either a Masters or a PhD, and so many others among the "educated" may question my qualifications to have arrived at my conclusions. Neither have I been a "lecturer" whose opinion is relished by the public as gospel.

Irrespective of that, I have two lessons that are necessary to state at the very beginning since all that follows will be based on these two lessons. Here is my lesson one: I have studied the conclusions of many who are much more educated than me or who are well-known by the public and find little relationship between these credentials and their ability to arrive at conclusions that hold any veracity. So always weigh what you see and hear and, after sufficient self-analysis, trust your own conclusions above all others, but be open to changing your mind if new knowledge or experience convinces you differently.

Here is my lesson two: the purpose of my life is to find objective truth and personal happiness. It is not to make another person happy at my expense, nor is it to endure suffering to achieve a higher level of being. It is true that my personal happiness may be enhanced by doing something for someone else to improve his/her way in life, but it certainly will not improve my goal towards achieving happiness if it does not come from my heart and mind. You will also notice I did not mention another's truth because there can be only one objective truth that applies to all and my goal is to search for it (logically, if there are two or more "truths" on the same principle than only one or none of them can be true. Truth is objective and absolute and is not synonymous with "opinion", which, of course, can be subjective and relative).

There are three "Letters". Each letter begins with a basic principle. Webster's defines a principle as a rule, guideline, precept, or law, so this word meets my intent. Each letter will expand on the principle and become more specific to include my own life experiences so you can better understand how I arrived at the principle. Some will agree with me. Others may not agree with me or even accuse me of arriving at a false conclusion. For you, I refer you again to lesson number one in the preceding paragraph. Since this is my writing, I will exercise my privilege to come to my own conclusions. There may be some specifics that you don't know about me that will come out. But they will only come out to better understand my life. Other things will remain within me. Names will be used and situations will be as accurate as I can recall. The purpose here is not to praise or condemn, but to share with you, my children, some important people and events in my life that framed my life experience and, thus my philosophy.

So let me begin with Letter One.

LETTER ONE: TO MY CHILDREN

*"The search for truth is true religion,
and the man who is seeking truth is the only religious man."*

Krishnamurti
Think on These Things

FRANK A. RUFFO JR.

THERE IS CONCLUSIVE EVIDENCE THAT THE UNIVERSE IS VAST AND COMPLICATED AND EARTH IS ONLY A MINUTE PART OF THE UNIVERSE BOTH IN SCOPE AND TIME.

The universe is so vast, so old and so complicated, I reason that there had to be an Intelligent Designer. So far, we have not scientifically proved this, and, we likely never will. A person is free to practice or not practice any faith that does not harm individuals or society. Organized religions have good and bad aspects, but none can be proven to be the work of a Supreme Being and therefore, none are essential for belief in God or participation in any after-life if such exists.

Fortunate to be in the latter half of my sixth decade of life, I have concluded that I have learned a lot and actually know very little. Since this appears to be a contradiction, I will need to explain, and my religious education and ultimate conclusion regarding religion are great examples of what I mean. I hope this is clearer to you by the end of this letter. So let me tell you about my life as it relates to the formation of my beliefs.

EARLY YEARS
(1942-1956)

As a child, my life was fairly simple, particularly from a religious standpoint. Like almost all recently immigrated or first generation Italians of that day, my parents practiced Roman Catholicism. My father was particularly religious, and remained a devout Catholic to his death. My mother seemed to go along with the faith because it was the "thing to do" more than anything intrinsic in her beliefs. My folks sent me to Grant Grade School, a public school, rather than the local parochial school, St. Patrick's, presumably, because of money though I never knew why and didn't care. Grant, being a public school, of course, did not teach any religion. As a result, I learned little or nothing about religion or God, except through observation.

And frankly, my observations created an aura of mysticism and outright fear of God. Father (Fr.) Anthony Buffaro, the Italian priest of St. Rita's Italian parish in Tacoma, was like most priests of that day: very strict, his word was the law since he represented Jesus (the Son of God), and he could somehow change bread and wine into Jesus' body and blood through Mass, which in those days was said in Latin facing the alter. So, unless you had a daily missal to follow in English what he was saying, you were lost. Actually, I had no interest in what was going on so I sat there and followed the requirements of the ritual, including sitting, standing, and kneeling in lock-step with the congregation. And by the way, kneeling was the longest and most agonizing, but Mom always made sure I kneeled without resting my rear on the pew seat.

In any event, the whole ritual coupled with the statues, alter, communion ceremony (which I was not eligible to receive since I hadn't as yet had my first communion), and the fact God was looking down at me with jaundiced eyes just plain scared me.

Since I went to a public school, when I was about eight years old my folks (mainly mother) did the obligatory thing and enrolled me in Saturday morning catechism. I think this was suggested by Father Buffaro as a requirement to participate in the "First Communion Ceremony". At my first session, the nun teaching the class called on me to stand and recite the prayer "Hail Mary", which of course, I didn't know. I started by saying "Hail Mary, full of grace—", and stopped, since I knew no more. Sister Mary Katherine (or whatever her name was) told me very tersely to sit down and that I didn't know anything.

I must have gone to two or three more sessions when, with great relief, I no longer attended. I have no idea why not except I must have satisfied the requirements for my first communion or Mom and Dad got tired of taking me. In any event, I have little memory of my first communion ceremony except that I was nine while everyone else was about seven, (one was supposed to have their first communion after reaching the age of reason which was presumed to be about seven. Just think of all those eons I would have spent in Purgatory if I had died before the ceremony).

My first confession was to Father Buffaro. I must have been taught how to confess my sins by the Sister Mary Katherine. I was scared out of my wits while standing in line to go into the confessional, and rehearsing the introductory prayer—"Bless me Father for I have sinned, etc." I counted up all my sins since the beginning of my life and finally arrived at the correct numbers. "I told lies 55 times and didn't mind my folks 65 times." Those were the only two sins I remember (those were the days!). The rest of my pre-teens were very innocuous, although I think I continued to occasionally lie and disobey Mom, and probably went to confession once in a while to cleanse my soul.

After finishing the sixth grade at Grant Grade School, I was looking forward to going to Jason Lee Junior High, where they had rotating classes and, of course almost all my friends were going to attend. I remember one friend named John Graham, who, although he went to Grant, had become an altar boy. So sometimes after school I would go over to his house and we would practice saying Mass, using fruit juice instead of wine. I still had no idea what it was all about except in a "real" Mass, the bread and wine became the body and blood of Christ.

John seemed very religious and he apparently decided to go to the seventh and eighth grade at St. Patrick's, the local Catholic school for grades one through eight. Since our folks knew each other, Mom thought it would be a good idea if I went to St. Pats as well. So during the spring of my sixth grade year, she took me to the school to register me for the seventh grade.

I was very intimidated by the nuns and, of course, was not looking forward to next fall. Anyway, to make a long story short, I put my foot down and refused to go. Apparently, I must have thrown a real fit, because my folks relented, and I started the seventh grade at Jason Lee that fall. John went to St. Pats and I didn't see him again until high school.

Jason Lee Junior High School was an interesting experience for me to say the least. I will talk more about this in another letter but, for this letter, the two instances I can recall that relate are my confirmation into the Catholic Church and my introduction to Father Jack Sneeringer.

Confirmation was another mystery to me. At mine, the Archbishop of the Seattle Diocese presided because of the apparent importance of this event. We were lined up on the communion rail at St Rita's and the Bishop anointed us on the forehead with some kind of oil. This ceremony is apparently a strengthening of the rite of baptism which I know I received as an infant. It was meant to bring us more in line with the beliefs of the Church.

Confirmation, St. Rita's Catholic Church (me, top row, second from right)

I was 14 (and in the eighth grade at Jason Lee) and turning into a little hoodlum. I was confirmed with about 50 others who also went to public school. We were all about three years beyond the standard

Catholic School age for confirmation. Prior to the actual ceremony, we were required to take an oath which, among other things, made us promise not to consume alcoholic beverages until we reached the age of 21. No way could I agree to that since my father had exposed me to wine at a very young age as part of our Sunday dinners (mixed with water, of course). Believe it or not, I didn't like it, and much preferred milk with our Sunday pasta. My father, being in the beer distributing business also exposed me to beer, which, at that time, I also could take or leave.

Anyway, when it came time to take the oath, me and Ernie Carino, another friend who was in class with me, crossed our fingers while ostensibly agreeing to it, signifying that we were not bound by that part of the oath.

The confirmation was on Saturday midday in the spring of 1956. In keeping with the anointing that I had just received, that night I went out with a childhood neighbor friend, Dave Peterson, and some friend of his named Paul. Dave was about three years older than me and, I think Paul was about three years older than Dave. They both were driving age so I went with them to cruise around Tacoma (sitting in the back seat). They had a bunch of dirty pictures of women and guys doing all kinds of sexual things, which I looked at. Although I was very curious of them, since I had never seen anything like them before, I felt guilty being mesmerized by some of those pictures.

At the end of the evening, we went to a drive-in hamburger place on 6th Avenue in Tacoma where girls served you at your car. It was called the Dugout Drive-in (no longer there). After waiting too long for our food we all concluded we didn't like the service our waitress had given us.

So as we drove out, I gave her the finger through the window. Unfortunately for me, her boyfriend was there. He happened to be a Tacoma motorcycle cop on duty and, when he saw my symbol, he immediately chased us down and pulled us over. He read the riot act to all three of us, made them take me back to apologize, and then escorted us to my house where he introduced me to my parents at our front door and explained what I had done. Needless to say neither of the guys were happy with me nor were my parents. I don't remember the exact punishment given to me, but it certainly created a memorable confirmation day, and showed my deep devotion to the Church in those days.

The second situation was my introduction to Father Jack. One weekday evening the same spring as my confirmation, my folks invited Fr. Jack Sneeringer, a priest from Bellarmine High School, to dinner at our house. I was intimidated by priests as much as nuns, so I was rather quiet during dinner.

After dinner, we retired to the living room. Here is when the main purpose of Fr. Jack's visit came to light; and that was for me to attend Bellarmine next fall for the ninth grade. That was a total surprise to me since all my friends were in public school and I thought I would complete the ninth grade at Jason Lee before going on to Stadium High School. I pleaded with my folks to finish Jason Lee and then consider Bellarmine in the 10th grade, but Fr. Jack convinced them that it would be much better for me to start the 9th grade at Bellarmine.

Contrary to my throwing a fit like I did when I was registered at St Pat's, I reluctantly went along with it. I'm not exactly sure why, but my mother always compared me to my cousins, John, Joe, and Ron Gallucci (Johnnie, Joey, and Ronnie in those days), and how they all went to Bellarmine and were straight "A" students. Also, besides the obvious academic success of my cousins, who were all valedictorians of their class, for the first time, given some of the characters that I met at Jason Lee who were deemed as part of "in crowd", I began to believe there had to be a better way (sadly, many of that in crowd either ended up dead or in serious trouble with the law before reaching the age of 20).

One of the requirements of Bellarmine was an entrance exam which I took shortly after Father Jacks' visit. Amazingly, I passed it easily; in fact I was told I did extremely well, much to my delight. Therefore, next fall was to be my matriculation at Bellarmine.

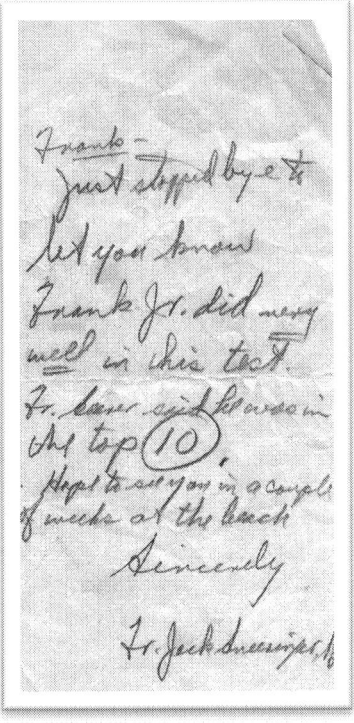

Note from Fr. Sneeringer to Dad

This was a major turning point for me and, I believe, paved my way for a real opportunity for a successful and happy life.

HIGH SCHOOL
(1956-1960)

The summer of 1956, I met Gene Pentimonti, whose parents had a summer place on Horsehead Bay, very close to our summer place in Moorelands. Gene had gone to St. Pat's so, although I had heard his name, I had never met him. We met at the local store (the Arletta store) by accident when both of our parents were shopping. That fall, on the first day of school, Gene was the first person I saw at Bellarmine. Although I didn't know it at the time, this would turn out to be a lifelong friendship (I will be discussing family and friends in another letter). I also found that I knew quite a few others in my class, having played little league sports with, or against, many prior to high school (Don Moore, Steve Anstett, Dick Henderson, Bob Hovee, Jim Schindler, Al Prentice, Bill Ehreth and, of course, John Graham from grade school, and my cousin, John Ruffo).

Bellarmine was a totally different experience for me. It was my first experience in an "all boy's school" and discipline was very strict. There were a total of about 300 students, and our principal, Fr. Christy McDonnell, ran the school as if he were a prison warden. I met several scholastics (Jesuits that were studying to be priests), and a couple of them became friends and I would see them off and on until they both passed away when I was in my late 50s-early 60s.

At Bellarmine, I was scared to death of failing since at Jason Lee, I received great grades with no homework requirement. Not so at Bellarmine. I spent hours at night studying. Although I had several subjects (English, algebra, Latin, ancient history, and religion), this letter's focus is on religion.

We were required to take religion every quarter from freshman to senior year. Not having had any formal religious education to speak of, everything was new. The course was straight forward, and black and white. I learned there were mortal sins and venial sins. Mortal sins would deny you salvation in heaven, but venial sins only required you to stay in purgatory until your soul was cleansed. There were obvious mortal sins such as murder, etc. but I also learned eating meat on Friday was a mortal sin as was not attending Sunday or Holyday Mass, unless you received a dispensation from a priest. I learned such things as French kissing, petting (not to mention sexual intercourse) and masturbation were mortal sins. These "sins' of the flesh didn't seem important then since I really hadn't started dating yet and had no clue what masturbation was. There were other sins that could be either mortal or venial, such as telling a lie, disobeying your parents, depending on the gravity of the behavior.

I learned that God was an all-knowing, all-loving, all-powerful being who sacrificed his son to save mankind from original sin (of Adam and Eve), and reopened the gates of Heaven through Christ. I learned that the Catholic Church was the only true Church and one had to accept this in fact (or somehow receive this knowledge after living a perfect life that would make him a Catholic anyway). We learned many other things about the Church, its history (believe it or not, the Jesuits taught about the Church evils of the middle ages, but believed it was all corrected). I already knew that a priest had the power to forgive sins in the sacrament of penance (confession). As a result of this training, I started going to confession and receiving communion, and became a strong adherent to the teachings of the Catholic Church of that day.

About half way through my freshman year, having become a scholar in the Catholic Religion, I started a discussion on religion with my public school neighborhood buddies on the front porch of our Cedar Street house. I explained to them that the Catholic Church was the only true Church based on Jesus saying to Peter (who we learned was the lead Apostle and first Pope), "Thou art Peter and upon this rock I will build my Church".

Being raised either as Protestants or without any religion, they, of course, would have nothing to do with my "preaching" and totally disagreed with anything I said. Anyway, I learned a lesson there, and never brought the subject up to them again (as a side note, as I became more involved with Bellarmine, my friends began to shift to those in my class, and I saw much less of my old neighborhood friends).

In my freshman year, I joined the St. Francis Sodality and was a member for three of my four years at Bellarmine. The mission of the Sodality was a special veneration of the "Virgin Mary", and I became prefect (president) of the group my senior year.

By my sophomore year, I had begun to experience "girls" and although I still had little "carnal knowledge", I started to become more interested in them. We had many school dances with the Aquinas and St. Leo's High Schools, the two all-girl high schools and dancing "close" to some of them became a "special" experience.

Throughout my high school days, I was very fond of the overall education I received, but found myself 'conflicted' many times by my behavior and the teachings of the Church and the priests. As an example, I frequently ate meat on Friday. And starting my junior year, I dated non-Catholic girls for no particular reason other than I had met them during the summers while living at our beach place.

At one co-ed high school retreat (retreats were required attendance and were organized to be two to three days of reflection, meditation, and praying) lead by a Dominican Monk, a student in the audience asked the Priest "how you could kiss your girlfriend without committing a sin". The priest answered, "Like your 80 year old grandmother." That answer was not acceptable to me or to my classmate friends. We decided that the priest had no idea what he was talking about.

I generally found that to be true in many discussions with priests, relative to appropriate behaviors and dating. During the summer prior to my senior year, I met Pam, a girl who lived close to our beach place, and we starting dating regularly. I ended up "going steady" with her for five years, through all of my senior year and college years. In all that time, we never had sexual intercourse (not that we didn't want to, but we were concerned about the impact on our lives if she became pregnant). So we resorted to what was called "heavy necking and petting".

During those days, our hormones were in full bloom. Initially, I would feel guilty after some of our escapades, but the guilt subsided as our relationship grew. Consequently, even though I was a member of such a group as the Sodality, by my senior year, I rarely went to confession because it still created the same trauma for me that it had with Fr. Buffaro at St. Rita's years earlier. So I began practicing a double standard and that seem to bode me well at that time.

The other thing Bellarmine was noted for was its strict disciplinary standards. The principal, Fr. McDonnell, carried a strap under his cassock, and had a yellow strip in front of his office for giving hacks to those who were disobedient. Bellarmine also had a program called JUG, which stood for Judgment under God. This was staying after school to do labor around the campus for rules infractions.

Although I believed in the concept of discipline, and accepted it as a fact of life in those days, today, it seems like the emphasis on discipline was not only counter-productive, but counter to the teachings of Christ, which is what the Church purported to represent.

I graduated from Bellarmine in 1960 and was accepted to The University of Santa Clara, also an all-male institution, to commence in the fall. Although my doubts about many teachings of the Church remained, I was grateful to have the Jesuits as educators.

During the summer of 1960, my relationship with Pam was strong. However, our relationship was not viewed with great fondness by either her folks (they softened considerably as our relationship continued) or at least one Jesuit Priest who had befriended our entire family, Fr. Joseph Penna, S.J. I remember a large family party at my Uncle Rick's beach house in Rosedale. Since we were eating outdoors and sitting at the same picnic table, I introduced Pam to Fr. Penna. He had the gall to ask whether she was right-handed or left-handed (which meant is she a Catholic or non-Catholic)? I replied, "Left-handed", to which Fr. Penna said to get rid of her. I was furious and we quickly finished our meal and left the gathering.

COLLEGE YEARS
(1960-1964)

In summary, I have had a formal education in the Jesuit tradition, studying all the standard requirements for receiving a degree including English, history, mathematics, (and theology, as required in a Jesuit setting) and received a bachelor's degree in Psychology with a minor in Philosophy. When pursuing these, like most students of my day (and, I expect any day) I had no clear goal in mind, but after having failed my attempt to pursue a pre-med degree at Santa Clara, which was Mom's desire, due to marginal grades, I switched my major to Psychology when I transferred to Seattle University.

Entering Santa Clara the fall of 1960, I was once again required to take religion (now called theology). We were also required to take philosophy and the first course was logic. Although I continued to practice the religion (primarily out of fear and guilt, and perceived peer pressure), internally, I increasingly started to doubt the veracity of many of the Church's teachings. Externally, I continued to attend Mass, and occasionally went to confession, and sincerely tried to pray (as I had in high school). By adhering to the practices of the Church, I felt good about myself, stayed in good stead with my folks, many of my friends, and, of course, virtually all my relatives.

However, by mixing science, logic and subsequent philosophy courses with theology courses, I became even more conflicted internally. Interestingly, over the course of the next few years, this remained my religious status quo, externally practicing and even criticizing those who didn't believe (even though I was becoming more doubting).

During the summer of 61, Joe Gonyea, a good high school friend who went to Santa Clara with me, was married (I was his "best man"). Prior to their marriage, Jo-Mae, his wife-to-be, converted to Catholicism, with me acting as her Godfather. I mention this because it obviously didn't take a saint to act as a Godfather (Interestingly, although Joe was 19 and Jo Mae was 18 when they married, they had four wonderful children, and are still happily married with a now large extended family, and are strong practitioners of the Catholic faith to this day).

*Me as best man, Gonyea Wedding, September 9, 1961
(Pam, second from left)*

My junior year in College (1962), I transferred to Seattle U, ostensibly because Santa Clara had gone co-ed, and I could continue my education in an already coed school closer to home. The real reason was I was still in love with Pam, and I wanted to be closer to her. But the point is, I continued the rest of my college career pretty much the same way, attending Mass, trying to pray, living the double standard and continuing to doubt much of what was being promulgated.

In the early 60's, certain things happened in the Church which were well-intentioned, but cast even more doubt. Under the questionable concept of "Infallibility of the Pope", the belief that as the Vicar of Christ on earth, the Pope, could make pronouncements in matters of faith and morals that were binding on the laity, the Second Vatican Council came out with new Church practices and laws. Among those that I recall were: meat could now be eaten on Friday with limited exceptions, confession could be conducted on a congregational basis rather than sins being forgiven on an individual basis in the confessional; Mass was now said in the vernacular (language of the land) and the priest now faced the congregation; attendance at other denominational ceremonies was no longer a sin.

I'm sure there were others but the point is that for me it furthered my belief that the Catholic Church was a man-made institution rather than promulgated by God.

In the late summer of 1964 I broke up with Pam (cowardly I might add) because I knew I was likely going into the Navy when I graduated and I didn't want to have her or me tied down during the years I would be gone. I graduated from college at the end of fall quarter, 1964, so technically I was in the class of 1965, and had been accepted to Officer Candidate School (OCS) at Newport, R I. where I entered class in January 1965.

NAVY YEARS
(1965-1968)

I will talk more about my Navy experiences later. Focusing on religion in my Navy career, I happened to meet many Catholics throughout my career, and most practiced "on again and off again". A couple of friends who I still stay in touch with continue to practice to this day (Jack Cannon and Mark Mahaffey). I had my moments of piety, but for the most part, stayed ambivalent to the religion, only occasionally attending Mass.

One exception was a period of time on the "*USS Bennington*". While we were in the Western Pacific, I met a Navy Chaplain named Fr. (Lieutenant Commander) Anthony Maritato. He was a great guy and always pushed for us to go to Mass. Mass always seemed to have meaning to me in an emotional setting or when there was a great sermon. And, Mass in the forecastle on the aircraft carrier while at sea in enemy territory, with air operations being conducted above, was definitely an emotional setting. But even then, I went through periods of considering myself a practicing Catholic and others where I didn't, but I almost always felt guilty when I didn't practice (commonly known as Catholic guilt).

MARRIAGE AND DIVORCE, ETC.
(1968-1985)

This subject also belongs in another letter regarding "family", but I will discuss these aspects as they relate to religion here.

In November 1967, I met a lady on a blind date that would become my future wife and the mother of my children. Her name was Joanne Reynolds, a native of Long Beach, California, which was my home port. I was due to be released from active duty in May 1968, if I didn't augment (which meant extending active duty and possibly becoming a member of the regular Navy, as opposed to the Naval Reserve). Joanne and I were still dating by May and, in part, because of this, I made the decision to go through with my release from active duty. We became engaged about the same time and decided to be married in August 1968.

Joanne in her Long Beach home, 1968

Of course the issue of a Catholic wedding came up, and Joanne, raised as a Methodist, would be required to take instruction in the Catholic Church and agree to raise any children as Catholic. We met the Pastor of the local Parish; as I recall his name was Fr. Flanagan. He was a great guy and extremely liberal relative to Church marriage rules. He agreed that we could be married with a Mass and Joanne could receive Communion at the ceremony. In the past, both were not allowed in a mixed marriage.

Anyway, Joanne took some instruction from him until late June, when we decided to spend the rest of the summer in Gig Harbor, Washington and find a place to live when we permanently relocated after the wedding (I had agreed to go to work with my father in the beer distributing business—in Letter #3).

We set August 10, 1968, as our wedding date in Long Beach with two receptions—one in Long Beach and the other in the Tacoma, Washington, area. We were scheduled to return to Long Beach around the beginning of August for wedding preparations. After about three weeks living with my parents in our summer place, Joanne elected to return to Long Beach. I returned to Long Beach a couple of weeks before the wedding to find out that Fr. Flanagan had left the Parish (word was he left the priesthood and married).

Fr. Kolberg, the Priest that replaced Fr. Flanagan, at first refused to have the wedding "blessed" with a Mass, and to have Joanne receive communion. After considerable pleading and arguing that Fr. Flanagan had already agreed to this, he reluctantly relented (for all I know, he needed to get permission from the Archbishop of Los Angeles). The wedding went off as planned and we left for Gig Harbor and our honeymoon immediately after the Long Beach reception.

For a few years, our marriage was fine; we ended up moving from Gig Harbor to SeaTac; then from SeaTac to Edmonds; and from Edmonds to Everett. In each case, we joined the local Catholic Parish and attended Mass regularly.

After three years of marriage, Brian, our first child, was born on August 29, 1971. Dutifully, we had him baptized at St. Mary Magdalene Parish in Everett with my good friend, Gene Pentimonti, and his wife, Jean, as his Godparents.

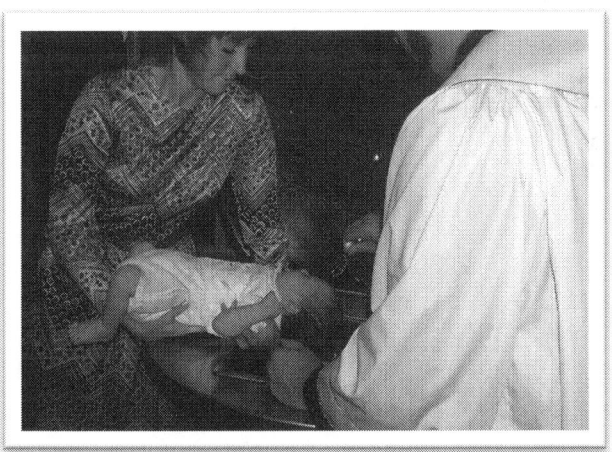

Brian's baptism with Godmother, Jean Pentimonti, fall 1971

In 1974, we moved to Federal Way. We became members of St. Vincent DePaul Parish, and it was during this period that Joanne converted to Catholicism (she was very impressed with Fr. Quig, the pastor). At that point we did attend Mass quite often and this period was a time where I really tried to practice my religion.

Christina, our second child was adopted two months after her birth which was January 19, 1977. She was baptized at St Vincent de Paul with another close friend, Mike Hosterman, and his then wife, Pam, as Godparents.

In 1979, we moved to Puyallup, and shifted to All Saints Parish. I still considered myself a practicing Catholic. However, over the course of the next few years, Joanne and I started having marital problems. She suggested that we attend a retreat that was in vogue at the time called "Marriage Encounter". Supposedly, it was designed to strengthen already good marriages.

We attended the weekend long session and after its conclusion, I outwardly praised and supported it and, initially, even thought it was helpful, but, ultimately, I came to believe it was a joke and designed to make everyone love and hug each other and generally "feel good". Anyway, it certainly didn't do what it purported to do for our marriage, and communication between us got worse and my commitment to the marriage continued to wane.

In 1981, while on a business trip, I met a beautiful girl, 12 years younger than me (I was 39 and she was 27). Her name was Jeannie. Jeannie was an administrator for one of our Midwestern facilities and I was required to travel there many times for business reasons. This was obviously not a good situation for either my career or my marriage, but I really fell for her. The relationship lasted about two months whenever I was in town, but then I realized it was futile to continue after my business ended, so I broke it off. The day I was scheduled to fly home for the last time was truly a sad day for both of us. We sat by a lake holding hands, then Jeannie took me to the airport, and that was it.

Back home, I felt that Joanne and I had developed a parent-child relationship with me as the child! I began to dread coming home every night and was thankful that my role at the Hillhaven Corporation required considerable travel. At this time, I also began to question many teachings of the Church and began to drift away, and out of a feeling of obligation, attending Mass only occasionally.

Because of my previous "affair", I was not myself around Joanne, and she sensed it. On one particular Sunday, although we were members of All Saints Parish in Puyallup, Joanne wanted to attend Mass at our old parish in Federal Way, St. Vincent DePaul. We sat in the front row. While Mass was being said, Joanne suddenly stood up and bolted out of the church sobbing. I knew that she had guessed that I had been involved with someone. I remember praying very hard for the remainder of the service, and I decided that if she asked, I would tell her the truth.

After Mass, I approached the car where she was sitting in the passenger seat. When I got in, the first thing she asked was if I was having an affair. I told her that I had been involved in a relationship in the Midwest, but that it was over. She started yelling at me and hitting me on my shoulder. When we got home she left the house for three days without telling me where she was going. I later found out she went to stay with some close friends of ours who had moved to Mukilteo, Washington.

When she returned, at Joanne's request, we started counseling, both having separate counselors. Joanne's was a Jesuit priest and mine was a divorced woman who was a very strong Catholic and also a very good counselor. Her name was Kathy and she taught me a lot about relationships and why some work and others don't. After many sessions of counseling, I came to the conclusion that I no longer wanted to stay married to Joanne, but I still stayed with it, probably from a combination of Catholic guilt regarding divorce and my perception of the reaction of my relatives.

Although I hadn't made any decision regarding divorce, on November 11, 1983, Joanne and I separated and I moved into an apartment in south Puyallup. Suffice it to say, this was a very difficult period in my life, although I was much happier on my own in the apartment. I was concerned about Brian who was 12 and Tina who was six, but I saw them frequently since I lived reasonably close to them. The one thing for which Joanne and I can both take credit is our commitment to our children. Although we continued counseling sessions, I never regained the commitment to make the marriage work. In fairness to Joanne, I think she was more willing to try than I. Anyway, about March or April of 1984, I filed for divorce. After about a year and a half, in July, 1985, after considerable struggle, our divorce became final.

SECOND MARRIAGE
(1985-TO PRESENT)

While I was separated, I started dating Sandy, a beautiful woman I met at work. We hit it off immediately and I fell big for her. This no doubt contributed to my total loss of interest in ever going back to Joanne. In any event, Sandy was to become my future wife, but here again the Church raised its ugly head.

In order to satisfy my guilt over the divorce and my perception of the wishes of my strong Catholic relatives, I filed for an annulment of my marriage so I could remarry in the Church. We also found out that Sandy, my wife-to-be, would have to seek an annulment, since her first marriage was in a Methodist Church, it was viewed as a Christian marriage. Although she was remarried a second time, that marriage of 12 years was not viewed as a legitimate marriage, because, according to the Church, her first marriage was still binding.

Although my annulment went through fairly quickly as well as Sandy's to her second husband, her first marriage posed difficulties. This was unbelievable; for, it required Sandy to bring back many negative feelings over old relationships and, in the case of her first husband of one month, she had to recall his cruelty and physical abuse to her. She also had trouble locating him and, when she did, it was a problem to get him to cooperate. Nonetheless, after about a year, the Church, in its wisdom gave her an annulment from both previous marriages.

Anticipating that the annulment process would go smoothly for both of us, we set our wedding date of May 2, 1987, in the chapel at Bellarmine High School. However, because of the difficulties for Sandy to receive an annulment from her first marriage, we realized that she would not receive it by our wedding date. At that point, and with Fr. Joe Maguire's blessing, we decided to have the wedding in our home on Shaw's Cove by Horsehead Bay, and then Superior Court Judge, Don Thompson, conducted the ceremony (Don, being a practicing Catholic, conducted the ceremony with the understanding that a priest would marry us when Sandy's annulment was final).

During the spring of 1988, the Church finally granted Sandy her annulment. We then contacted Fr. Joe Maguire, regarding conducting a Catholic ceremony at the Bellarmine Chapel on May 2, 1988, exactly one year after our civilian marriage. Unfortunately, that date was taken so we settled for May 1.

So on May 1, Fr. Joe conducted a marital Mass in the Bellarmine Chapel with only my children and my parents present. Now it was "official" in the eyes of God! That being said, we still celebrate our official wedding day as May 2, 1987.

Our "Church" wedding, Fr. Maguire

The family at our "blessed" wedding

Sandy's and my marriage was (and is) wonderful. Oh, we had some rocky times, primarily over my violent reaction to the loss of my senior position at Hillhaven, but we made it through it all. Regarding religion, even though we lived in the Arletta, Horsehead Bay area, a considerable distance from the Catholic Church, we did attend Mass quite often. Sandy never converted but would receive communion with me. We particularly liked the Pastor at St Nicholas in Gig Harbor, Fr. Bill Lane. But then he left for health reasons and his replacement was terrible. We tried going to St Charles in Tacoma, but eventually stopped going altogether, except with my mother during holidays (holy days) or to attend funerals.

During this period, a couple of things occurred that I have not forgotten. Our friend, Fr. Joe Maguire, was dying of cancer, and on my last visit to see him, I asked him what he thought about Catholicism, Jesus, etc. His response, "It's a myth, but a good myth. And I'm at peace."

I will never forget those words. For, what I think he was telling me is that as human beings we can know very little of the supernatural so we must tell stories to describe it as best we can.

Fr. Joe's words provided me with my missing link and helped me to solidify what I believe today.

The second thing that happened and continues to happen today is how a parish priest can dictate which attendees at Mass can receive communion. As I mentioned, Sandy, a non-Catholic, regularly received communion when she attended Mass. A priest named Fr. McDermott, had taken it upon himself to decide who can receive communion, and specifically announced at every Mass that, "Practicing Catholics can receive communion." I presume he had decided that any non-Catholics who may be devout Christians are still unworthy "to receive".

Well, Fr. McDermott, you were the last straw as far as I'm concerned. You also helped me in my beliefs in your own misguided way, and I thank you for that. It also solidified that Catholicism, as well as all other religions are man-made. And that brings me to the present and to a dissertation of my beliefs and why.

PHILOSOPHY AND CONCLUSIONS

As Krishnamurti said in my quote at the beginning of this letter, I am in search for truth. After all the teachings and experience related to religion, I see no merit in subscribing to any of them. Some conclude that there is a Designer and a First Cause (although some try to distinguish between a Designer and a First Cause, unlike the proofs for the existence as articulated by Thomas Aquinas, I will use the term "Designer" to signify both). For many, natural logic concludes this when you observe the creation, wonders and intricacies of our universe. Beyond that, all else is conjecture that may be based on faith, myth, emotion, hero worship of someone else's beliefs, or a need to cling to something outside of one's self. For others, there is no proof that there even was (or is) an Intelligent Designer. For me, I have no clue either way, but do marvel at the wonders of our existence and conclude this could be based on nature, evolution and natural selection or the work of an Intelligent Designer or some combination. No one has ever offered any verifiable proof that either a Designer or First Cause does or does not exist.

My Jesuit training did teach me one thing and that was "how to think". Over my life, I have given this matter of God as much thought as any other subject. I have concluded that there are too many unanswerable questions to believe on Faith alone that there is or is not a God (Designer). We do have the tremendous gift of the ability to think and it seems like a crime not to use it. So I will now summarize some of those questions and why they are bothersome to me.

First of all, the religious texts that have been written do have historical value to understand the beliefs that existed at the time the writer composed them. Many of the messages in the Bible (Christian), the Koran (Qur'an, Islam), Torah (Judaism), Book of Mormon, Trip Taka (Buddhism), Veda (Hinduism), and others are worthy of reading and understanding because the message they send in many cases can be great for humanity. Yet, other messages are filled with hell, damnation and hundreds of years of torture and death. In any event, there is no proof that they are divine works. They are books and not the word of any Divinity translated through a human mind. Many advocates of each book will disagree, but their beliefs are beliefs only and are not based on any verifiable proof. The mere fact there are so many books about what is true is telling in itself. Either only one is true or none are true. I suspect the latter.

The principal subjects of these books are Jesus, Mohammad, Moses, Moraine (revealed through Joseph Smith), Gautama Siddhartha (Buddha), the Aryans, and others who, like them, have had a revelation from God (or an inner spirit). I do not quarrel with their beliefs, but I conclude that there is no way we can know that what they preach are truths or divine revelation. They may have been prophets of their day, but that is my only conclusion.

There are modern day and ancient teachers, preachers and evangelists, who firmly believe in their teachings (and some who are profiteers who only preach for monetary gain). There are others who write books proving that their prophet is the divine leader, i.e. Lee Strobel, C.S. Lewis, and St. Paul regarding the divinity of Jesus to name a few in the religion in which I am most familiar. However, their beliefs are based largely on biblical interpretation, and it can be shown that the Bible is filled with many flaws, particularly when comparing the gospels and the disparity of time frames between events and the different depiction of events in Jesus' life from one Gospel to another. It's not my purpose to explain these here, but if you have an interest in understanding the specifics, I suggest reading "The Age of Reason" by Thomas Paine or viewing the four hour PBS series "From Jesus to Christ" which is available on the internet.

History teaches us that various Councils formed long after Jesus' life and the lives of the writers of supposed Holy Scripture actually decided what would and would not be included in the Bible. Also, until the 7th century, any written word was in Arabic, Hebrew or Latin and only the educated could come close to reading it, books were scarce and only portions were translated into English. The first complete English translation of the Bible did not occur until the end of 14th century by an English theologian named John Wycliffe. Other translations were made between 14th and 16th centuries. And today, if one visits Borders or Barnes and Noble, there will be a section filled with various printings (i.e. King James, the Catholic Bible, American Standard Bible, the New American Catholic Bible, etc.). With so many different translations and inclusions and exclusions as to what is Holy Scripture, which one is divine? Or all they all divine? Or none of them?

For those who do believe the Bible is divine and are members of an organized religion that regularly attend Church or prayer services, I suggest reading The Gospel of Matthew, Chapter 6, verses 1 through 8. Here, Jesus seems to be saying not to attend public gatherings or pray in public. "Be on guard against performing religious acts for people to see — When you are praying, do not behave like the hypocrites who love to stand and pray in synagogues or on street corners in order to be noticed. —Whenever you pray, go to your room, close the door, and pray to your Father in private."

"Food for thought?"

Theological history is replete with legalisms to control an unthinking flock (the Faithful), total misconception and outright untruths. To name a few: the earth is flat; the earth is the center of the universe, the sun revolves around the earth; the Catholic Church is the "One True Church"; the Pope is Jesus' representative on earth; the Pope is infallible; it is a mortal sin to eat meat on Friday; the "mysterious concept of the Holy Trinity" (that is three Persons in one God), etc.

Many of these thoughts point specifically to the Catholic Church, but all other Christian religions are off shoots of the Church and therefore, at the very least, espouse that Jesus is the Son of God (based on Faith alone and no verifiable proof except as a "post-diction" rather than a prediction that he would and did rise from the dead. And that post-diction was written many years after the supposed event occurred).

Some deny the existence of any Designer and say they can prove it as well i. e. Richard Dawkins, "The God Delusion". Dawkins bases much of his premise on the Theory of Evolution which is well known and promoted in Charles Darwin's book, "the Origin of Species", written in the mid nineteenth century. However, the argument here is that the opposite of evolutionist theory is not creationist theory, as Dawkins and many Atheists would have you believe. On the contrary, I believe it is acceptable to conclude that a Designer designed evolution and evolved humans through the evolutionary process. It is completely logical to assume a Supreme Being had no problem allowing the evolutionary process to occur as part of nature. It is also theoretically possible to conclude that there is no Designer and the process evolves on its own (Although I agree with much of what Dawkins says about organized religion, his precepts do not prove there is not a Designer).

Because of this, many proponents of organized religion believe they are forced to adhere to the theory that at some specific point, a Creator injected the human being into the world (stemming of course from the Old Testament, the Book of Genesis, in which God created Adam and Eve, another fairy tale). They are then required to deny evolution since they believe the two precepts are contradictory.

This is unfortunate, because I believe Darwin's theory has been demonstrated as almost a fact through geological, zoological and other scientific study over the last 150 years since his book was published. In fact, if one observes other primates from conception to adulthood, it is difficult not to conclude that we are very closely related and this process evolved as part of nature.

Another cumbersome mystery for me has been the question of good and evil and why certain people suffer and others do not. And, as for the power of prayer, I don't believe a Supreme Being can change the course of human behavior or natural events that cause injury, death and destruction because of prayer. That could not be part of God's nature, it defies logic and would show favoritism which can't logically exist in a perfect being. The fact that some prayers seem to be answered while others are not is pure coincidence and can't, by its very nature, have anything to do with any external maneuvering from God.

Man does have what has been labeled "free will". Therefore, he can freely choose to do certain things and not do others. Both absolute good and absolute evil exist, and rationale beings can discern one from the other. Therefore mankind is constantly faced with a conflict between good and evil and, on issues that allow choice, he can chose to follow either the good or evil path (or cop out all together by following the path of moral relativism).

Therefore, individual inner strength can develop from meditation and prayer. Individuals can become enlightened and the human body may react positively from that. Prayer used to gain inner strength to deal with events out of our control is beneficial. It may even help cure an affliction because of psycho/physical reactions in the body. But, to repeat, a Designer (God), by its very definition, cannot change outcomes for some and not for others even though they both pray or only one prays or neither of them prays. So, in our world, in issues where man has no say in the outcome, sometimes good seems to prevail and other times, evil does. Therefore, in these cases, prayer is useless for it cannot logically be in God's nature to listen to some and not others, assuming both are sincere in their supplications.

In a nutshell, I have studied the writings of Aristotle, Emanuel Kant, Voltaire, Thomas Jefferson, Benjamin Franklin, and Thomas Paine, who all searched for truth and concluded that if there was a God, He was very passive in nature. Like them, I see no absolute proof that one exists, only my physical observation of the wonders of the Universe. Although many of them who came to America during what is known as the Age of Enlightenment were obviously very familiar with the beliefs of the Church of England (and Thomas Paine was brought up in both Anglican and Quaker environs), in the end they practiced no organized religion.

So my children, I believe that whether Jesus actually existed or not, the written message is one of peace and is good for the soul and the message is essential for the survival of western civilization. Although Jesus may have been the Son of God as I was taught, there is no proof that he was what the Bible says, and because of all the discrepancies in the Bible, it is hard to conclude that it could have been the handy work of God. In fact, many theologians consider its contents based largely on myth. Therefore, one certainly can and many millions do believe that Jesus was the son of God, but that belief has to be based solely on faith. So it is one of those beliefs that one can take or leave or leave as an unknown. I have chosen the latter.

Having said that, the message of Jesus is both inspirational and unique, and, for practitioners, can bring inner strength. The message preaches peace, forgiveness and love. Western civilizations used the message as a model for ions. Its moral and legal systems are based on it. This has been a good foundation for our Country and it must maintain this foundation (see section on politics). Our founding fathers were strong advocates of his message and so am I; whether one actually practices a Judeo-Christian faith is a matter of religious freedom as called for in our constitution.

Is there life elsewhere in the universe? Again, no one knows. However, we do know the vastness of the universe, how complicated it is and we can calculate with some accuracy for how long it has existed. Based on this, one can easily theorize that there has to be one or many more environs in our universe that did, does, or will sustain life. I believe that, but because of the universe's vastness, we may or may not ever see it while human life exists on this earth. But mankind will continue to explore and I hope we find the answer. To find life elsewhere will blow a hole in many of the teachings of organized religion unless Jesus or Mohammad could travel through time and space and we find the Bible in other worlds. But that is of no consequence to me. So we continue our search for truth.

What happens at death? No one knows. Again there is much speculation as well as those who believe they have seen revelations when having near death experiences. There are also those who believe that they can communicate with the dead and with Saints. There are those who espouse to be intermediaries to help one on earth communicate with deceased loved ones. There are those who believe in reincarnation, that they will assume another life or even another form of life to complete unfinished business that they had in their current life, and so on and so on.

None of these beliefs have been proven to be true. Therefore, I conclude these after death experiences to be either mere fantasy or one's mind, not truly dead, is deceiving the individual. I do hope that science will continue to explore and someday find more answers, irrespective of existing religious dogma or the proclamations of pseudo-scientists claiming to have proof of experiencing or witnessing a "divine event". In the meantime, it is obvious we are thinking (spiritual) as well as physical beings and, although I have no knowledge that there is life after death, I leave that door open. If there is, I will repeat the conclusion of Thomas Paine that "—at my death, I will rely on God to do with me as he will," and I have no idea what that is.

So, what can one conclude from all this? Well, as I said in the beginning of my letter, throughout my life, I have learned a lot, but I now realize I know very little. It comes down to this: there is a strong argument for an Intelligent Designer, based on the vast and complicated universe, but one could suppose it is possible the Universe in some form existed forever. Although our planet contains exactly the elements necessary for life and furthers the proof for an Intelligent Designer, it is also plausible that life, including intelligent life, will be discovered elsewhere.

I also see no conflict between mankind's evolving from other (lower?) life and the existence or non-existence of a Designer. On the contrary, it is also very likely evolution is a law of our universe and will continue to influence all objects, matter, and inhabitants. Whether evolution is the work of a Designer or is only a natural law will forever be unanswerable to us while alive in this form, because of the absolute irreconcilability of science and religion.

So there you have it, I have arrived at these conclusions, and from a philosophical, religious, or metaphysical point of view, that is it. So where does that leave me regarding my beliefs? From the studies and observations of science, we have learned a lot about our origin and likely outcomes. To me, these are our best definitions of truths we have today, based on the rigid verification requirements of the scientific method. It has also been shown that a just society serves itself well by incorporating Jesus's message of respect for a human life to maintain individual freedom.

And, at my death, as I stated, although I have no knowledge that there is an afterlife, I do have hope that there is one and that many of these questions will be answered. As a mere mortal I can only wait to see and, to be sure, I would love to experience myself continuing to exist in some form after death. Of course, if there is no after life, then there will be nothing.

I do have one prayer that I keep on my office desk that I believe says it all regarding our individual responsibility. It is also one that I have found to be personally challenging throughout my life. Here it is:

God, grant me the serenity
To accept the things I cannot change;
Courage to change the things I can;
And wisdom to know the difference.

Well, my children, this concludes my first letter. It is now time to close the chapter on the scientific, religious and metaphysical and embark on more practical, mundane and everyday happenings of living one's life. So on to my next letter.

FRANK A. RUFFO JR.

LETTER TWO: TO MY CHILDREN

"We hold these truths to be self-evident, that all men are created equal, that they are endowed by their Creator with certain unalienable rights, that among these are life, liberty and the pursuit of happiness."

Declaration of Independence
second paragraph

"No man is an island entire of itself; every man is a piece of the continent, a part of the main."

John Donne
No Man is an Island

FRANK A. RUFFO JR.

**TO ACHIEVE HAPPINESS
REQUIRES INDIVIDUAL FREEDOM.**

This means there must be a just and moral society with reasonable laws, a society that governs by distinguishing the difference between natural law and civil codes, and provides all with protections from inequality and tyranny.

By definition, a just and moral society must have a just and moral government. So this chapter will focus on our government, my exposure to it, how I view its history, the social, civil, and moral issues that our government has had to, and is, dealing with, and my conclusions regarding where we stand today.

SCHOOL YEARS
(1947-1964)

As a youth, I was ignorant of our government. The first President I remember was Dwight Eisenhower. It was the summer of 1952; I had just turned 10 years old, we were watching the Democratic and Republican conventions on our small black and white television at our summer beach place in Moorelands. The candidates were Adlai Stevenson, the Governor of Illinois (Democrat) and General Eisenhower (Republican) who was a hero during the Second World War. Eisenhower's campaign was centered on stopping the Korean War which had begun under Harry Truman.

During that summer, we wore "I Like Ike" buttons. I must have received mine from my parents. My folks were independent voters; they made their voting choices on the basis of who they liked rather than any ideology or political platform. For example, my father knew Al Rosellini, the Democratic candidate for Governor (he was Italian). It really didn't matter whether he was a Republican or Democrat. This was how they voted for all levels of government so I grew up thinking that the most popular guy won (in fact, name recognition is paramount when one is in the voting booth).

During my high school years, our school closed early one afternoon so the entire student body could walk down the hill to Union Street (now Avenue) to wave and cheer as President Eisenhower came by in his motorcade. Although the event had a memorable impact on me, it didn't create any interest for me in politics or the government.

During the summer of 1960, John F. Kennedy and Richard Nixon (who was Eisenhower's Vice President) were elected by their respective parties as their presidential candidate. This turned into a not-so-friendly campaign, particularly because Kennedy was a Roman Catholic. Since I was a Catholic, I paid some attention to the race. So did many at Bellarmine High School, a Jesuit school, as well as many non-Catholics who I knew, including Pam, my high school sweetheart, and her family.

Pam's family was very much opposed to Kennedy because of his Catholicism. They believed that if Kennedy became President it was the beginning of a government takeover by the Catholic Church. They had also heard that the Church was building up an arsenal at Mt. St. Michaels Abbey in Spokane, Washington, for that very purpose. How preposterous, but it shows the religious discrimination of that time. In any event, we all know that Kennedy won the election as the youngest President ever elected to the office and the first Catholic. I was not yet voting age although if I was I would have no doubt voted for Kennedy solely because of his persona without knowing either candidate's platform.

When the Kennedy family moved into the White House, the place was labeled as Camelot. I never really knew why (Kennedy's classmate at Harvard, Alan Jay Lerner, had penned the hit song "Camelot" for the Broadway Musical and it was a personal favorite of Kennedy; his favorite lyrics, "Don't let it be forgot that once there was a spot for one brief, shining moment that was known as Camelot"); if he only knew how clairvoyant he was regarding his brief presidency.

When I was a freshman at Santa Clara University, we were afraid of having to go to war because of the disastrous Bay of Pigs invasion in which Fidel Castro prevailed over a force organized by our CIA. During the next year and a half the Soviet Union built missile bases in Cuba and during my junior year at Seattle University, Kennedy successfully forced them to dismantle the bases.

On November 22, 1963, about 11 AM, I was taking a philosophy exam when we all heard a lot of commotion in the corridor. Then someone shouted that President Kennedy had been shot. I wasn't quite through with the exam so I tried to concentrate on finishing it along with my other classmates (Fr. McGuigan, our philosophy professor did confirm to us that Kennedy had indeed been shot). We all know the rest of the story, but virtually any adult of today knew exactly what they were doing or where they were at that moment.

November, 1964, was the first Presidential election in which I was eligible to vote. The candidates were Lyndon Johnson (Democrat) and Barry Goldwater (Republican). It was at this point in time that I started developing my own political philosophy. It was apparent to me that President Johnson, who replaced Kennedy when he was assassinated, believed in big government. I voted for Goldwater, who believed much government responsibility should be vested in each State, as was the intent of our forefathers when they framed the constitution. Johnson won by a landslide and during his State of the Union address he outlined his "Great Society" plans. Subsequently, he won passage of major legislation, including civil rights, anti-poverty, aid to education and healthcare (Medicare and Medicaid), resulting in a major increase in the size of our Federal Government.

Before my time, Franklin Roosevelt's "New Deal" was the first major expansion of Federal Government's power since the founding of our Nation. Roosevelt can be credited with introducing us to deficit spending for public works, asking, and receiving emergency powers to greatly expand the government's regulation of business, passing an excess profits tax, implementing a progressive income tax that produced a redistribution of wealth on an unprecedented scale, and instituting the Social Security system. Roosevelt realized the danger of unions infiltrating the public sector and, therefore, opposed it (unfortunately, his opposition has not prevailed in our day). The expansion is widely credited for saving our Nation from the depths of depression, although I believe our entry into World War II provided a substantial boost for the economy. The mobilization of our Nation to join with our allies and fight a war on two fronts and win both wars was a major accomplishment for which he deserves full credit, although he did not survive to see the victory.

NAVY YEARS
(1965-1968)

To this day, President Johnson is praised by many for his "Great Society" policies. Although the 1964 passage of the Civil Rights Act (which he was politically forced to do) was long overdue, I opine that his continued expansion of the government and his handling of the Vietnam War was an atrocity for our Nation, the negative effects of which are still with us because of the philosophy inculcated in the minds of many of our 1960's youth, who now play a large role in government policy.

My first incident involving government ineptness and military bureaucracy was taking over the collateral duty of Supply Officer on the "*USS Pluck*" (unlike most Navy ships, minesweepers were too small to carry a full time Supply Officer so a Line Officer was assigned the duty). Shortly after assuming the responsibility, I became suspicious of my storekeeper, Miller. Officers were required to pay $44.88/month for their meals and Miller was responsible for collecting the fee and turning the funds into Long Beach Naval Base. Based on my review of Miller's records, I became concerned that he was pocketing the money rather than turning it in.

The next month, I set up an entrapment in conjunction with the naval base's disbursement office. After Miller collected the monthly funds, I waited a reasonable number of days for him to turn them in. I went to the disbursement office and he had not yet turned in the funds. Astonishingly, the office had no record of him turning them in for several months.

I immediately reported the matter to Captain Leopold, who in turn took it up with the base commander. A couple of days later, Captain Leopold told me that the base commander wanted Miller to face a court martial. The Captain then told me to hire my own attorney because he also wanted to court martial me for assuming legal responsibility for the department and having this thievery occur under my watch.

I could not believe it; the government at its best. I catch the thief and they want to court martial me because I was the officer in charge. I immediately called my father who suggested I contact my Uncle Al who went to law school with the assemblyman (congressman) for Los Angeles County, Vince Thomas. I did just that and Uncle Al and I jointly spoke to Assemblyman Thomas so I could tell him my story. Assemblyman Thomas said he would look into the matter.

Within a few days, Captain Leopold called me to his cabin to tell me that the base commander had decided only to continue with the Miller court martial.

"Lesson: clout works!"

It was 1966 and there was little resistance to our presence in Vietnam, although that would all change as we escalated the conflict under President Johnson. Anyway, our MSO (ocean minesweeper) squadron of five ships shipped out in May as scheduled (See Navy Years in Letter #3).

Upon arrival in the Philippines, I was transferred to the Naval Hospital because of a stomach ulcer and, what was also diagnosed as chronic sea sickness. I spent most of July and August attached to the

Hospital—first as an inpatient; then for the majority of the time, as an outpatient.

Here, was my first exposure to anti-war sentiment regarding our role in Vietnam. While in bed at the Naval Hospital and unable to talk because of tubes placed through my nose to my stomach to test my stomach acid, an aviator entered my room, changed to a hospital gown, and occupied the bed next to me. The next day my tubes were removed and we introduced ourselves.

I learned he was from Texas, and was hospitalized because he refused to drop his bombs over North Vietnam, claiming the war was unjust and we were killing innocent civilians. We were both discharged from the hospital at the same time and moved to the BOQ (Bachelor Officers Quarters). We spent several days together visiting Manila, Corregidor, etc., until he was given a Section 8 general discharge (mentally unstable) from the service and sent back home to Texas.

For the next month or so, I had virtually nothing to do and I was becoming increasingly agitated at the Navy for apparently forgetting about me. I tried to contact my father by telephone, but found it impossible to do since all communications were prioritized and mine was considered routine. I finally was able to get a letter approved to send to him. Within a week, I received a response from Dad that he had contacted both Senator (Scoop) Jackson and Congressman Floyd Hicks. Shortly after that I miraculously received orders transferring me to Oakland Naval Hospital for a medical evaluation.

"Clout again!"

Upon arrival at the Oakland Naval Hospital, I went through a medical evaluation and was found fit for duty (which I had wanted). I was given temporary orders to report to the Naval Engineering Group based in downtown San Francisco and to move to the BOQ on Treasure Island.

It was here that I saw the dissention that existed in our country over the war. I taxied it back and forth every day between Treasure Island Navy Base and downtown. It was summer, so I would always wear my officer khaki uniform. One evening while sitting in the back of a taxi and stopped at a red light waiting to proceed onto Interstate 80 across the Bay Bridge to TI, a disheveled guy with long hair approached my taxi and spat at me through the open window on the passenger side back seat where I was seated.

I could not believe it and was tempted to leave the vehicle and take care of the idiot right there. However, the taxi driver, being wiser than me, encouraged me to stay in the vehicle and made many snide remarks regarding "hippies" in San Francisco. The light turned green and we proceeded onto the bridge.

I was TAD (temporary duty) in San Francisco for about six weeks and every night, heard on the news stories of demonstrations against the war in San Francisco and anti-war demonstrations spreading to other metropolitan areas and college campuses throughout the nation. Being a loyal member of the military and based on their anti-violent protests coupled with the drug use and free sex culture of the hippies, I became very intolerant of them and, in those days, actually had no problem with our government (or other citizens) doing whatever with them.

In November of 1966, I received orders to report to the aircraft carrier, "*USS Bennington*", based in Long Beach California. Shortly after reporting aboard, we set sail for the Gulf of Tonkin off the coast of North Vietnam.

Just prior to sailing through the Hainan Peninsula entering the Gulf, we received intelligence reports that we were to be confronted by North Vietnamese sampans lining both sides of the entrance. They were armed with 50 caliber machine guns which would be pointed directly at us. As the officer of the Deck at the time, I asked permission of the Captain, Richard Graffy, to blow them out of the water. Since President Johnson would not let us shoot unless we were shot at first, Captain Graffy refused, but ordered me to make turns for 30 plus knots. I sent the order out to the six destroyers accompanying us and we entered the Gulf safely, hopefully with our fleet's monstrous wakes sinking some of the sampans in the process. What a great war we were fighting with our government tying our hands behind our backs!

We visited the Gulf three times during that deployment for 60 days, 45 days, and 30 days respectively. We were deployed from November 1966 to June 1967 but were relieved of our Vietnam duties in May. We returned to Long Beach where we home ported until I was released from active duty in May 1968. In August, 1968, I married and returned to Washington State where I stayed in the reserves for about seven more years.

CIVILIAN LIFE
(1968 - PRESENT)

The years 1968-1970 were transition years for me. Our country was in a total state of disarray like we hadn't likely seen since the Civil War. On March 31, 1968, President Johnson announced he would not seek reelection for which I was delighted.

On April 3, 1968, one of my high school friends and college roommate, Jack Brady, was ambushed and killed while on a scouting mission in South Vietnam. Jack must have been clairvoyant because the prior New Year, I was home on leave and Jack held a large New Year's Eve party at his folk's home shortly before deploying to Vietnam as an Army Second Lieutenant. In conversation that evening, he said that he likely would not return from Vietnam alive. After hearing of Jack's death, I was extremely distraught, but I still had faith that our country was doing the right thing in Vietnam.

Jack Brady, high school friend and college roommate

On April 4, 1968, Martin Luther King was assassinated in Memphis, Tennessee. Actually, I was somewhat ambivalent about his assassination, given my early background where my surroundings and associations were almost totally with whites and blacks in my area were generally treated as second class citizens or viewed as hoodlums that should be avoided. However, his assassination ultimately gave me pause and I began to focus more on why. I remember driving down Anaheim Boulevard in Long Beach in my Corvette that evening with mob violence developing in the street. Out of fear for my life, I gunned the vehicle and ran several red lights thinking if I stopped I was history.

After my release from active duty in May of that year, I remained in Long Beach until mid-June. On June 5, several of us were in my apartment watching the California State victory rally for Bobby Kennedy in Los Angeles when we heard shots and saw Bobby fall.

He died shortly thereafter. Another assassination was hard to fathom and made me very distrustful of the whole process.

After moving to Washington State, given my military background, I still disliked the whole counter culture movement and the anti-war demonstrators. In late August, 1968, the Democratic Convention in Chicago turned the City into total chaos with mass riots where demonstrators were intent on disrupting the Convention by any act whatsoever, including the use of violence, both organized and unorganized.

I remember watching the convention on TV and rooting for the cops and hoped they would annihilate all those anti-American hippies. In fact, in anticipation of the violence, in addition to the cops, the US Army, the National Guard and the Secret Service were called in, and, in some cases, they had to use considerable force to control the mob (and it was a mob).

The 1968 election resulted in Richard Nixon, who campaigned on ending the Vietnam War, defeating Hubert Humphrey, who vowed to continue Johnson's policies. I voted for Nixon (parenthetically, even though Nixon won with a landside of electoral votes, the popular vote was very close and, of course, my own State of Washington was the only Western State to support Humphrey. This would be an omen for me personally; with few exceptions, I have been at odds with my own State politically except Ronald Reagan on virtually every election beyond the local level since then).

After Nixon was elected, things seem to quiet down for a while because of his campaign promise to end the war, but the war dragged on into 1969 and 1970. Nixon even escalated it by announcing that he was going to bomb Cambodia. Predictably, the anti-war demonstrations resumed in full swing, mainly on college campuses. The culmination occurred on May 4, 1970, when Ohio National Guard troops opened fire on Kent State student demonstrators killing four students and wounding nine others. Over 1.2 million students demonstrated. Nixon further exacerbated the problem by calling the demonstrators bums.

Through all this, I continued to support our military and our president. In a discussion with several colleagues at work we all felt the college students got what they deserved. I continued to support our military and our government to the end of the Vietnam War, which occurred in August, 1972 when our combat troops exited Vietnam (Saigon didn't actually fall to the North Vietnamese until 1975).

On the domestic front, Nixon dealt with several issues. I will focus on three that still impact us today. First, the creation of the Environmental Protection Agency in December 1970. The EPA was one of the first agencies to deal with a social issue and today it has spread to be one of the most powerful movements in our country (who hasn't heard of endangered species, going green and global warming/climate change). Unfortunately, this was a new type of legislation without any boundaries or accountability. As a consequence the EPA and its Federal, State, and local government offshoots that now exist have gained virtually unlimited power with no over site and it is considered a sacred cow today which no politician will touch. I will elaborate further on this at the end of this chapter.

Second, under Nixon, the dollar was taken off the gold standard which caused the value of the dollar to fall (that was the intent because of inflationary pressures abroad). This resulted in a substantial increase in inflation to 6-7%. As a result, on August 15, 1971, Nixon imposed wage and price controls to try to stem inflation. It simply didn't work and, in fact, by mid-1974, the inflation rate reached double digits. It dropped drastically under President Ford only to rise to its zenith under President Carter.

Third, in response to the United States resupplying Israel during the Yom Kipper War (against Palestine), in October 1973, OPEC plus Egypt and Syria imposed an oil embargo. Nixon reacted by issuing an order rationing fuel to 10 gallons every other day (determined by odd/even license plate numbers), and lowering the nation's speed limit to 55 miles per hour. All of us remember the long lines to fuel up, but by March 1974, a settlement was negotiated and Israel withdrew from the Golan Heights, ending the oil embargo (but oil pricing became the new monetary standard which is in full force today [my words]).

In June, 1972, the Watergate scandal began and over the course of the next two years, unbelievable facts began to unfold regarding our government's illegal and downright criminal acts. It became clear to me that all of this was President Nixon's doing and many of his followers were brought to justice. It was then that I began to rethink my position and loyalty to our government.

When Nixon resigned in disgrace in August of 1974, I was just as relieved as I had been when Johnson chose not to seek reelection. I also liked Gerald Ford and knew he would replace Nixon, but when he pardoned Nixon, he made a terrible political mistake. It ultimately cost him his election to the Presidency and our Nation voted in Jimmy Carter as President.

Domestically, when Iraq invaded Iran, the result was a drastic decrease in the oil supply which resulted in another shortage causing the second oil crisis of 1978. To Carter's credit, he initiated a National Energy Policy that decontrolled domestic oil prices. However, under Carter's leadership, by April 1980, we saw the highest inflation rate ever seen in the US. He terminated the wheat program to Russia, he turned the Panama Canal over to the criminal Panamanian government (Manuel Noriega), and did nothing about the Iranian Revolution including interceding in the Iranian hostage crisis (these were American citizens!). Although, he placed considerable emphasis on the environment and on human rights, he couldn't overcome the high inflation rate and seemed weak in his efforts to free the Americans who were held by Iran. I personally did not like Carter. I viewed him as a mediocre leader, and was delighted when he lost to Ronald Reagan in a 1980 landslide.

"American strength in unity!"

It took a President like Ronald Reagan to restore my faith in the office of the President. I have to say Reagan was by far the best president so far in my life, for these reasons: He loved America! He loved what our forefathers believed and created, and he tried to re-instill this in our Nation once again. He believed in small government (although he was less successful in shrinking it), and believed that government doesn't solve problems; it is the problem.

During the 1980s while Reagan was president, the Iran hostages (52 Americans) were freed on the day he was sworn in, the Soviet Union began to teeter under pressure from his administration who labeled it "the evil empire"(it ultimately fell under President George H.W. Bush), the income tax code was modified with much lower tax brackets that exempted the low income, interest rates began to fall, he broke the air traffic controllers union when they tried to hold the nation's air transportation system hostage, and he created a strong military. I respected him for all of these feats, although he was never successful in controlling deficit spending.

For me, the 1980s decade was a period of professional growth and success, and with relative peace and posterity in the world, I had little criticism of our government throughout the entire period. I was gratified to see that even my own state of Washington supported me and voted for Reagan in both 1980 and 1984.

George H.W. Bush, who was Reagan's Vice President, succeeded him in 1988. Bush was a distinguished naval pilot during World War II and had a great track record as a student, entrepreneur, and member of Congress and head of the CIA. He was not as dynamic as Reagan but he was a good President and, as all presidents, had several issues to deal with, including the first Iraq War (in which he gained support of the American people and many nations due to Saddam Hussein's invasion of Kuwait). My state reverted back to its old habit and threw its electoral votes to the Democratic candidate, Michael Dukakis.

I did become more interested in politics during Bush Senior's re-election campaign in 1992. His popularity had waned largely because he violated his campaign motto, "Read my lips; no new taxes!" (which he violated in a compromise with the Democrats), and the economic downturn with the S & L crisis. The reason the campaign was something to watch was because Ross Perot, another Texan, had joined the race as an independent. The Democratic candidate was Bill Clinton.

I was torn between Perot and Bush, but, in the end I voted for Bush, believing that Perot's candidacy would split the ticket more in favor of Clinton than Bush. I was correct; Bill Clinton was elected with 43% popular vote to Bush's 37.4% and Perot's 18.9%. Perot won no state's Electoral College vote, and, as usual, my State of Washington voted against my Bush vote for the Democrat, Clinton.

A high priority for the Clinton Administration was health care reform. President Clinton put his wife, Hillary, in charge of completing the plan. As we know, her efforts failed, due in large part to the mass opposition from insurance companies, doctors, the American Medical Association, and the public at large. Clinton's attempt at health care reform (including universal health care for all) occupied much of the first two years of his first term, and ultimately caused a mid-term election loss of both houses for the Democrats for the first time in 40 years.

At the time Clinton was President, I did not care for him for these reasons: He acted like a glad-hander (a phony); he supported and ultimately succeeded in passing, the Omnibus Budget Reconciliation Bill of 1993, which imposed a tax on the wealthy and a tax cut on low income wage earners; and most of all, his moral behavior and subsequent lies became public and made him unfit to hold office of the President of my country. During the two terms of Bill Clinton, by his own moral misbehavior and then lying about it, he became only the second President to be impeached by the House of Representatives (he was later acquitted by the Senate). It is also believed he should have focused more attention on taking out Osama Bin Laden, which he failed to accomplish, with disastrous consequences for the United States resulting in several terrorist attacks (e.g. responsibility for the *"USS Cole"* attack and, of course, the September 11, 2001 attacks).

However, after further reviewing his record and reflecting on his presidency today, I must say in retrospect, he can take credit for many laudable accomplishments including convincing the Democrats to support the Republicans in the Senate to ratify the North American Free Trade Agreement that was negotiated by President Bush (H.W.); focusing on the economy and the deficit which resulted in the first budget surplus since 1969, impressive economic growth resulting in very low unemployment and minimal inflation; opening trade with China; substantially lowering poverty among minorities, single mothers, and the aged; shrinking the welfare system; and negotiating the compromise, "Don't ask, don't tell" policy regarding gays in the military, much to the dissatisfaction of gay groups. Notably, many of these accomplishments can be credited to the 1994 elections resulting in the Republicans taking control of Congress. That said, Clinton left office with a 65% approval rating, the highest approval since Dwight Eisenhower.

Clinton' successor, George W. Bush, came into office because of Supreme Court ruling granting him the 25 electoral votes from Florida. He thus defeated Al Gore, the former Tennessee Senator, in a close and hotly contested election. I was pulling for Bush all the way, and he did win. As usual, my politically astute state threw its 11 electoral votes to Gore (and, of course John Kerry in 2004).

In my opinion, George Bush was both an excellent president and a mediocre president, depending on the issue (I must add, however, he was an honest, straight-forward leader; we always knew where he stood on issues). He led our Nation through the ordeal of 09/11/2001. He showed outstanding leadership by uniting us like we haven't been united since World War II. His support for the military and swift action against Al-Qaeda and the Taliban regime in Afghanistan was very well received by our citizens and the world at large. I was very proud to be an American and wished I could personally kill Osama bin Laden (and still do).

Even Bush's entry into Iraq in March 2003 was initially well-received by the majority of American people, based primarily on supposed intelligence data regarding Saddam Hussein's intentions and his regime possessing weapons of mass destruction (WMD). I was a strong advocate of the invasion and intensely watched it on TV in Phoenix while on a business trip with several colleagues, who were also very supportive. However, the intelligence was found to be in error, and as time went on, Democrats made political capital from this even though all had the same intelligence and almost all voted for the invasion.

The real problem was, initially, the Administration did not follow through on the war; they had developed no plan to win it. I began to vacillate on the reason we were still in Iraq. No doubt Saddam Hussein was evil, but he hadn't hurt us or our interests like he did by invading Kuwait in the early 1990s, while Bush's father was President. There is an argument that by invading Iraq we prevented further terrorist activity within the borders of the United States. But I began to doubt the validity of that argument. By midpoint in Bush's second term, I was tired of Iraq and thought we should cut our losses and pull out. However, prior to his exiting office, President Bush implemented "the surge", which seems to have worked so effectively that Iraqi forces are now capable of taking over military responsibility.

On the domestic front, Bush worked with the Republican Congress to pass a $1.3 trillion tax cut of which I was very supportive. However, this was viewed as primarily helping the rich, although it was intended to stimulate the economy (which it aided in doing big time, to the point that something was bound to give). He also pushed through the "no child left behind" initiative, which was written jointly by Bush and Democratic Senator Ted Kennedy, which received strong bi-partisan support and which I also supported. However, many states, including ours, have done a mediocre job of implementing the NCLB's educational standards.

On other domestic issues, he was very conservative and came close to interjecting religion into the government with his faith-based initiatives. In addition, because of the fear created by his War on Terror, Bush was able to form the Department of Homeland Security, pushed Congress to pass the Patriot Act, which was (and still is, as of this writing) viewed by many as granting the government massive powers to invade the privacy of individual Americans. I was very concerned over the use of these laws as a vehicle to contradict our constitutional rights.

Like many Presidents, Bush's second term became increasingly controversial, even from many allies. Both his world-wide and domestic popularity plummeted due to the Iraq War, his Administration's perceived inept handling of the Hurricane Katrina response (the facts will show the perception was wrong; Bush did all he could under the law; the real ineptness lies in the hands of the leaders of the state of Louisiana and the City of New Orleans, but only perception mattered), warrantless surveillance controversy, a lack of any immigration policy, record budget deficits, and the faltering economy. The American people showed their distaste in the 2006 mid-term elections by bringing the Democrats back to both houses of Congress.

During his last two years, immigration reform, Iraq and the economy became bigger issues. Bush acted like a "tax and spend Democrat" and when the economy started to plummet, he instituted the first government stimulus package. Anyway, by the November 2008 election, it was virtually impossible for a Republican President to be elected. As president, Bush received some of the highest approval ratings in American history as well as some of the lowest, and he left office as one of the most unpopular Presidents in history.

The campaign for the next president was largely in the hands of the Democratic Party since it was obvious to me a Democrat would be elected. It came down to a fight between Hillary Clinton and Barack Obama. Obama won the nomination based on his campaign of "change", his perceived oratory ability, and his sanctification by our media (who lost their objectivity about the same time as the counter culture movement of the 1960s).

As of this writing, Obama has been President for about a year and a half. To date, he has been a major disappointment. He has spent and spent to allegedly create a stimulus to pull the world out of the worst economic downturn since the great depression. I do agree he needed to bolster our financial industry to provide resources to rescue the economy, but he is doing more than that. He rescued many other institutions that had totally mismanaged themselves, first and foremost, the American auto industry.

In my recent past when I was still active in industry, I many times gave training seminars and used the American auto industry as an example of a coming complete failure. They still practiced the John Kenneth Galbraith economics of build a product and the consumer will buy it. Not so when they build a product of poor quality that the consumer will not buy. The American auto industry has been comprised of good-old-boy non-imaginative leaders who were so arrogant that they were incapable of learning anything from their competitors or anyone else. They were also subservient to the United Auto Workers Union so it was difficult to understand who really ran their companies. It is not surprising that all American companies but Ford (whose current CEO, Alan Mulally, came from outside the industry) went bankrupt and needed to be bailed out by our government (this was started under the waning days of the Bush Administration and vastly expanded under Obama).

President Obama spent virtually all of his first year on his campaign agenda with almost no regard for the real problem of joblessness facing the American economy. Specifically, both he and Congress made their highest priority his health care reform efforts and, it appears he has repeated the scenario of the Clinton Administration in the early 1990s. The American people once again vigorously rebelled against both him and Congress. This made no difference to either the President or Congress until an election in the state of Massachusetts created a massive political upheaval; the election of Republican, Scott Brown, to complete the remaining two plus years of the deceased Ted Kennedy's senatorial seat.

Although there were three state elections that should have said something to the President, he still kept his focus on health care reform. Because of the election of Senator Brown in Massachusetts, the Democrats were no longer able to invoke cloture in the Senate. Therefore, Obama was forced to make gestures toward focusing on the unemployment rate, but, rather than focus on solutions that were most likely to succeed, he continued his own socialistic, far left value system, which, in concert with his partners, Harry Reed and Nancy Pelosi, maneuvered healthcare reform through the Congress without one Republican vote (the first time in history a major bill was passed solely by one party), violating my principles of fair dealing, congressional protocol, and possibly, constitutional law.

"Change for sure!"

Although we have major health care reform as a matter of law, the process used to pass it was deplorable. And to exacerbate the divisiveness, this President who campaigned on uniting our country, on March 25, 2010, gave a speech mocking those who did not agree with his healthcare agenda. He was very arrogant and demeaning. He virtually demanded that Democrats in the House vote for the Bill, not because it was good for the country, but for his legacy. Certainly, this is extremely amateurish and not what I would expect from anyone who has the credentials to lead our country.

More recently, he showed his ineptness in managing the British Petroleum oil well disaster. After 50 some days of the well explosion and subsequent oil leakage into the Gulf, he finally said something to the American people and met with BP and other oil executives. His speech was a disgrace filled with platitudes and little or no emotion for the plight of our citizens in the Gulf. He has joined in with other members of our government in playing the "blame game", and explained to Matt Lauer on the Today show how he was going to "kick ass"!

This is a President? It is obvious he is totally inexperienced and incompetent. Yes, the problem was serious, very serious, but anyone with a minutia of executive experience knows that one has to gather the best minds in the field of expertise as quickly as possible to even attempt to tackle the problem. Yet he waited 50 plus days to do this.

In summary, President Obama is scary. I am concerned about his domestic agenda, his far left philosophy which, at its best, seems to promote a European-like socialism. He seems to believe that government is the solution to all problems—exactly the opposite of his hero, Abraham Lincoln, and certainly the opposite of Ronald Reagan. He is promoting a Robin Hood mentality that will rob form the rich (and, in my view, the successful) and give to the less affluent (which will increase the welfare state). I am also concerned his increased emphasis on Afghanistan is risky, although he apparently learned from George Bush and has put General David Petreaus in charge of "a surge" similar to Iraq. The War on Terror (or whatever the Obama administration chooses to call it) needs to continue against Al-Qaeda, but the Obama administration's approach has been weak. His administration is apparently more interested in protecting the civil liberties of the terrorists rather than protecting the American people.

To put it mildly, he has not shown strong leadership nor has he appointed able advisors in most of his Administration. If he continues this path, he will likely beat Jimmy Carter as the most inept president in our time. Because of these egregious violations and his arrogance, the future of many Democrats in both houses to maintain their seats and the ability of the President to carry out the rest of his socialist agenda will likely suffer the consequences. Although I favor a change to rid us of the current Congress, the change may result in a "do nothing" government for at least the next two years, which will certainly be an improvement over the "big government" policies of the last several years.

We are facing a continuing weakening of Abraham Lincoln's famous, "Government of the people, by the people, and for the people." With our current presidential and congressional leadership, it may well "parish from this earth" unless we stop it. President Obama's policies have infuriated the left, the middle and the right; his popularity is about to dip into the 40% level after only a year and a half in office (it took George Bush eight years to achieve that!).

Moving to other matters, it is extremely difficult to separate the government from the many social issues with which we are confronted today so I've chosen to discuss them. So here I go to discuss those issues that are important to me, not in any particular order.

ENVIRONMENTALISM

Let's begin with environmental issues. As I mentioned when discussing the Nixon presidency, the modern environmental movement began with the formation of the Environmental Protection Agency. There was a conservation movement throughout the 19th and 20th centuries. National Parks were formed and names like John Muir, Henry David Thoreau, Teddy Roosevelt espoused and /or practiced conservationism. However, I will make a distinction between legitimate conservationism which does exist to this day, and hype, conjecture, job creation, power, and inappropriate or unnecessary government control under the guise of environmentalism.

I will use two examples that had or are having a direct impact on me personally.

The first occurred shortly after Mom's death in September, 1999. My parents owned commercial property in Tacoma that had a drive-in restaurant, and two warehouses on the property. As executor of the family estate, I decided to sell the property. Since the neighboring business wanted the property, we negotiated a price and started the process of closing the deal. What I thought was going to be a straight forward sale turned into a nightmare.

As part of the due diligence to close the deal, the buyer, and his lender wanted a Phase One Environmental study completed on the property. The Phase One discovered underground fuel tanks adjacent to one of the warehouses. I did further research of the property file and determined that that particular warehouse had opened as a gas station in the early 1950s, but my father had closed the station and converted the building to warehouse use. The records further showed that he had complied with existing regulation at the time by emptying the tanks and filling them with clean sand.

I thought, "No problem. Dad complied with the law so it should be a done deal." Boy was I wrong! Because of the findings in Phase One, a Phase Two Environmental study was now required. A Phase Two involved soil sampling to determine if there was any contamination of soil, or, worse yet, ground water that might impact the environment.

In addition, the underground tanks needed to be removed. Underground tank removal fell under the jurisdiction of the local health department, which in my case was the Tacoma/Pierce County Health Department, whereas soil sampling fell under the jurisdiction of the State Department of Ecology (that of course was formed after the formation of the Federal EPA). So, here's what I had to do:

- Hire an environmental consulting firm
- Hire an environmental attorney
- Test the soil (the tests determined there was soil contamination around the tanks beyond the limits allowable by state law but no ground water intrusion)
- Remove and dispose the tanks
- Remove several tons of soil to an offsite location for cleaning it of contamination and replace it with clean soil
- Establish a pipe aeration system in the new soil so that over time, any remaining contaminates would dissipate

- And, finally develop a monitoring system to determine how fast the contamination was dissipating

The total cost to the estate was about $300,000. The property itself sold for $525,000 so that would have left a net of about $225,000, except for one piece of luck. Our environmental attorney asked if there might be some old insurance policies around that were dated prior to about the mid-1980s when Comprehensive General Liability (CGL) insurance policies didn't exclude environmental cleanup and thus, cleanup may be covered. Luckily, I found two policies and we contacted both companies. Of course, they initially denied the claim, but being aware of current law and after considerable negotiation, we settled my claim for about $100,000 from each company. So, the end result was a total out of pocket cost of about $100,000 to the estate—most of which was the cost of the tank removal not covered by any policy. After almost three years after mother's death, we were able to proceed with the sale of the property and close the estate.

As of October, 2010, example number two is still ongoing. As of this writing, I own a 60' boat slip at Murphy's Landing Marina in Gig Harbor. I have served on the Board and as the Marina Association's President three different times, each time for a two to three year period (I am the current president for the fourth time, because of my "expertise" in dealing with the government vis-à-vis the environmental issue). The Marina has an excellent harbormaster, Bruce Rogers, who has served us for the last 20+ years.

The Marina was built in 1986. As part of completing the marina, a berm was placed around the perimeter to minimize erosion being caused by a nearby creek and an adjacent city outfall. Periodically, our harbormaster would notice small breaks in the berm and gather a crew of marina owners to perform maintenance on it to repair the breaks. This had been the practice for 20 years until the summer of 2006. Apparently some environmental nut saw us working on the berm and reported us to the City. The City ordered an immediate cessation of our activities unless we were authorized to perform the work or face a substantial fine.

Of course we complied and undertook a study to determine what we needed to do to continue to maintain the berm. We were shocked to learn that we could no longer maintain the berm because it was determined that the nearby creek could be a habitat for Chinook salmon which was on the list of endangered species (steelhead were added in May 2007 to further complicate our project).

At the time, I was on the Board of Directors. The Board undertook the task of hiring a consulting firm specializing in berm repair and dredging, particularly because of increased erosion into the Marina basin since we were forced to stop the maintenance. With the advice of our consultant, we decided to make application to build a permanent berm and then dredge the Marina back to its original depth (which we can do under certain "grandfather" provisions). As of this writing, we still have not received approval to either build the berm or dredge.

Here's what we have been required to do and accomplished so far:

- We hired our consultant.
- We consulted with both environmental and land use attorneys.
- We had the marina surveyed twice to determine the amount of material estimated to be removed.
- We obtained approval to temporarily maintain the berm through October of 2009 during the okay months of July 15 to February 15 (when there is apparently minimal damage to fish because they aren't likely to be present) pending permanent repair. We were also required to report to the various agencies what repairs we conducted, including number of sandbags used and footprint covered.
- We conducted soil samples which have determined that the removal of the material is clean enough to be disposed by

barge in deep water rather than being required to dispose of it upland, which would have added major cost.

- We submitted our proposal to build the berm and dredge to the Army Corps of Engineers who is typically the lead agency in these matters. The Corps told us it will be at least a year before we will hear from them since several other agencies are involved.
- We were required by the City of Gig Harbor to seek a permit from them and pay the requisite permit fee for each step along the way.
- We were required to hire our own biologist who, on three different occasions, has had to submit a report of his findings.
- We were required by the City to notify residents within 300 yards of the project of our proposed action at least three times (every time we modify our project to satisfy an agency).
- We completed an archeological study since Indians once occupied the adjacent land.
- We will be required to do some mitigation to make up for any alleged damage we may cause to the habitat of the endangered species.
- As of August, 2010, we have now been ordered to obtain a water quality certification from the State of Washington and wait for the completion of a study by National Marine Fisheries (which is being completed by a person named Dave Molenaar, a bureaucrat, who has a reputation that is far from being unbiased and seems to be the actual decision-maker). The Corps is also requesting a complete environmental safety study of the vinyl material we are proposing for our wall (which I understand they have used in their own projects; ridiculous!).

In the meantime, the erosion continues. Since we can do nothing even on a temporary basis between February 15 and July 15, when the rainfall is the heaviest, the runoff from the City outfall continually breaks through the berm causing more erosion and damage. Our guest dock which is closest to the outfall is now almost dry at low tides to the point that it is starting to break up.

To exacerbate matters even more, here is a list of agencies that will need to approve the project: Army Corps of Engineers, US Department of fish and Wildlife, National Marine Fisheries Service, State Department of Fish and Wildlife, State Department of Ecology, City of Gig Harbor, and the Puyallup Indian Tribe. Presumably our consultant will work with the Corps to seek approval from the Federal and State agencies. And, all this because our own people have been prohibited from making ongoing minor repairs to protect our marina because we threaten to create so much damage to fish that one almost never sees at the base of our harbor. In addition there is a City waterfront park adjacent to our marina. The public walks on the beach, into the outfall, launches kayaks, all at will, but we are prohibited from even setting foot on the beach between February 15 and July 15. What a joke!

It is obvious we can't even go out for bid on this project until we know what the Agencies will approve. So, here's the bottom line. As of August 2010, although we received a denial of our application from Washington State Department of Fish and Wildlife, and a letter of Non-concurrence by National Marine Fisheries, we have worked out an informal agreement with the State which we can't submit until the Army Corps approves our application. As of this writing, we are still trying to obtain their approval for the berm, even though they keep putting blocks in front of us, including recently adding three more species of fish to the endangered species list and closing all marine dump sites for dredging material until the Corps completes a study. We will need to work through their reasoning to try to arrive at a solution that will protect both the "fish" and the marina (although National Marine Fisheries only cares about the fish).

Although we are hopeful we will work through their issues, it seems likely the project will not be completed before 2011 (or even 2012, if at all), five to six years after we began. As far as cost, we are only able to project total cost based on our consultant's experience elsewhere, so we are estimating a cost of about $1 million or about $13,000 per slip (85 total slips). We are assessing our owners with periodic payments to pay for the project, assuming we will be able to complete it as proposed.

"We're from the government; how can we help?"

These are two examples of a growing government bureaucracy that is causing us to lose our competitive edge, is self-serving, is out of control and is completely unnecessary for the well-being of the American people. I have heard it said that it is the philosophy of these agencies that the human element is the problem and they care less about the impact on human livelihood and individual property rights, but only focus on their mission which is to protect the environment and endangered species without regard to any human suffering, time lost and costs involved. And most politicians won't touch this issue at all. So, unless we as citizens do something, we are simply stuck with this nasty process and will need to practice adaptation until we tire of the impact on individual human beings and force action so we can stop this total outrage. We must all be stewards of our environment, but we must develop a legitimate partnership so regulations enacted to protect the environment (and endangered species) also include the impact on the human element.

Once again, I quote, "Government of the people, by the people and for the people". In this latter example, it is government for the fish alone without accounting for the impact on us.

"Justice, bureaucracy or agency totalitarianism?"

GLOBAL WARMING AND CLIMATE CHANGE

Although this subject is closely aligned with environmentalism, because of its unique emphasis, I have chosen to discuss it separately. I am not a scientist and don't profess to be one. However, I have a strong interest in scientific issues and have studied many of them since I was a child—particularly astronomy/cosmology and now, climate change.

First of all, there is certainly not universal agreement among the scientific community on global warming as a fact and even more uncertainty regarding a human causal connection. That is why I believe the concept of global warming has now been labeled "climate change", which is much easier to sell to the public at large without complete agreement among scientists. Secondly, the issue not only raises important environmental concerns, but also broad political and economic consequences (and opportunities to capitalize immensely in both arenas). Thirdly, it is a very emotional issue with conservatives generally not believing that it even exists, but rather, temperature fluctuation is a natural phenomenon that has been occurring for eons with little human influence; and liberals believing that mankind is largely responsible for global warning due to human-caused increases in greenhouse gases in the atmosphere which is raising the CO^2 (carbon dioxide) level, thus warming the world climate and melting the polar ice caps with forecasted disastrous consequences.

In the absence of definitive and relatively universal scientific evidence to the contrary, I tend to side with my own conservative position (by this, I mean "safe"; not automatically buying into the politically conservative position). Simply stated, I see evidence that climate change is occurring.

With that conclusion, I believe we are approaching this issue too hastily, and, as a result, we are increasing our chances of totally missing the mark. It is a fact that irrespective of global warming, more flooding damage will occur. Why? Because many more people are living on the coasts for its attractiveness, and in many areas we are well aware that we are not equipped to handle the effects of a natural occurrence (i.e. New Orleans and Hurricane Katrina). It has been argued that global warming has resulted in an increasing number of violent storms and/or droughts. Really? I suggest you look at a yearly history; you may be surprised in spite of what some high profile people say (Al Gore?).

I will site one organization as an example of promoting immediate solutions for climate change. There are many other so-called "green" organizations that espouse similar philosophies.

Greenpeace, an organization on the forefront of fighting human-caused global warming has much of its existence wrapped up in convincing the American people and the world at large that this is true. If you look at their web site, one can't help but buy into their stated mission and goals. This is particularly attractive to many young people. Greenpeace has been in existence since 1971 (parenthetically, the originators had sound motives as strong advocates of conservation; they have long since left the organization because of its shift towards radical environmentalism).

Rather than promoting critical analysis and further Research and Development on the climate change issue, they have stated that one of their top goals is, "Catalyzing an energy revolution to address the number one threat facing our planet: climate change." How do they know it is the number one threat? And if it is, will an energy revolution solve it? What kind of energy revolution will solve it; promoting the elimination of internal combustion engines; turbine engines? Expanding the use of bio-fuel, or battery operated vehicles?

Greenpeace has frequently disrupted legitimate projects that have little or no harmful impact on the world i.e. blocking nuclear submarines entrance into port under the guise that the spent nuclear material is harmful. Greenpeace is opposed to the use of coal as an alternative to oil; is promoting the banning of all incandescent bulbs in the world and replacing them with compact fluorescent bulbs; is opposed to nuclear power as an alternative energy source, and opposes further drilling for oil—any of which would make us more energy independent, and much of it can be accomplished with minimal environmental impact.

As a result of efforts of organizations like Greenpeace, most politicians (including George Bush, John McCain, Barack Obama and most of the rest), many businesses, educators and college students are buying into the program. In vogue today is the use of renewable resources. We now see an ever-increasing "going green" movement, expansion of bio-fuel, hybrid vehicles, the use of fluorescent bulbs (CFLs, which are neither as environmental-friendly nor have the same capability as the incandescent bulb, although they do use much less energy), solar and wind energy to name a few.

Although we are doing some oil drilling, the emphasis is clearly not there (and off shore drilling is very much opposed by the environmental movement, and, no doubt, the recent BP disaster in the Gulf will exacerbate this). We all know that President Obama has energy policy as a high priority during his administration. I agree with his objective, I disagree with his motive. It should be not to solve climate change (which could prove to be a natural phenomenon), but rather to be less reliant on fossil fuel and thus foreign oil. I support expansion of nuclear power, massive oil exploration, both inland and off shore, and the use of clean coal and natural gas, of which we have abundance. I also believe we can accomplish all of this in an environmental-friendly way without the need for a large government police force to oversee it. So-called "cap and trade" is a bad idea and, thank God, there appears to be little support for it irrespective of President Obama and various world environmental groups.

In summary, have we done enough research to determine if the time and money spent on alternative energy will reduce enough carbon emission to make a difference? Or will a reduction in carbon emissions solve the problem at all? I'm all for less reliance on imported fossil fuel and for developing reasonable alternatives to fossil fuel in general, but the question is if we eliminate its use by 10-30-50-100% will it matter vis-à-vis climate change? We may be focusing on the wrong problem and, even if it is a problem, the wrong solution or there may be no solution, which, if true will prove very profitable for the few, very costly for taxpayers/consumers, and a monstrous waste of time.

This is one area where we should follow the advice of Jim Collins in his book, "Good to Great", where he quotes the CEO of Walgreens, a very successful drug store chain, "We're a crawl, walk, and run company". Shouldn't we approach this massive issue of climate change in the same way? As an example of an unworkable (and silly) approach to solve a serious problem, we know that there are several thousand deaths annually caused by auto accidents. There is a simple solution to bring this number close to zero. Lower the speed limit to 10 miles per hour! How reasonable is this? Regarding the environment, we should still be in the "crawl" stage. That certainly means practicing conservation, but the government needs to be cautious about imposing solutions that are unproven and may hardly help achieve the goal and, at the same time, cost a fortune and loss of livelihoods. Appropriately, as in other innovation, the private sector is taking the lead (and risk) to develop solutions.

"Government, stand clear!"

If proof someday concludes that man had little impact on climate change, rather it's more a natural phenomenon, we must ask ourselves how we can use the change to our advantage. There are those who believe that global warming will give us the ability to feed more of the world, will help us eradicate age-old disease like malaria, and to substantially decrease the poverty level of the world.

Anyway, it's in your hands and the hands of the generation that follows you. And contrary to those naysayers who have panicked the nation, in many cases for ulterior motives (fear, money, power, control), I believe you do have time to verify the scientific research and crawl, walk, then run.

ENTITLEMENT PROGRAMS

Woodrow Wilson expanded the practice of having a central government to solve human problems, in direct contradiction to the intent of our Founders. However, prior to Franklin Roosevelt, government entitlement programs were virtually non-existent. Because of the "Great Depression", Roosevelt was able to pass his New Deal which provided some relief for the 25% unemployed in the country. As part of his program, he also passed Social Security, which was an insurance program meant to provide basic sustenance for the retired.

Since Roosevelt's time, we all know there have been an increasing number of entitlements, including post war GI bills, Medicare, Medicaid, prescription drug programs, many "grant" programs, etc. My point is not to explain each entitlement program, but rather to point out that these programs have become about 60% of our national budget and together with interest payments on our national debt, Congress only has about 20-25% of our actual budget for other programs, including the military. Therefore, the only way to pay for all this is through borrowing money, printing more dollars, or increasing taxes. The last time we had a surplus was under President Clinton. Under President G.W. Bush our national debt skyrocketed, mainly because of fighting two wars, and because of the passage of the Medicare Modernization Act, signed in December of 2003 and implemented January 1, 2006. This Act, which provided drug coverage for seniors, was the biggest change to Medicare in 40 years. Although I was in favor of Bush's $1.3 trillion tax cut, it doesn't seem to jive with these massive spending programs.

Once an entitlement program is implemented, it is virtually impossible to abolish, with increasingly devastating effects on our economy. Unfortunately, our politicians from both parties don't seem to care. Under the current administration (Obama), Congress has spent a year to pass a massive healthcare reform bill (labeled "Obamacare"). This bill has now passed and was signed by President Obama on March 23, 2010. This new law will cost the American taxpayer well over a trillion dollars (forget the $950 billion figure released by the CBO) and purportedly would increase coverage for 31 million Americans. Since the language in the plan is so massive, few in Congress read it before its passage. The majority of Americans believe the plan is flawed due to its cost, added burdens to the States, and the requirement that all must purchase health insurance (violation of our constitution?) or face a fine. It will further increase government bureaucracy to fully control 16% of our GDP. Obama and his congressional cronies, Reed and Pelosi, have succeeded in jamming this massive entitlement program down our throats, through secret meetings, sleazy dealings, and threats.

All Americans are indebted to the people of Massachusetts for electing Scott Brown, a Republican, to replace the seat vacated by the death of Senator Kennedy. This election alone has shifted the balance of power so that any Democrat who supported this crazy bill faces the risk of being voted out of office. Meanwhile, our economy continues to struggle and unemployment is high. Obama's argument was that the bill's passage was necessary to reduce the cost of healthcare. This is pure gobbledygook! Most Americans understand this is a flat out lie. Any additional entitlement program has to increase costs. The only way to reduce the cost is to modify the existing program by allowing national competition among private insurance companies, require the insured to pay more of the premiums and choose the coverage they want, just like any other kind of insurance. This reform must include tort reform to reduce the high cost of malpractice insurance which is discouraging entry into the medical professions. Of course, this law includes none of this!

"Thank you legal and insurance lobbyists!"

My point is, the entitlement mentality that has developed among our politicians and our people has got to change, or we will continue our regression towards socialism like Europe and, even worse, the former Soviet Union. That will take leadership that apparently is non-existent today, so my children, here is another challenge for you and the generations to follow you.

Remember this quote from Thomas Jefferson, "A government that is big enough to give you everything you want is strong enough to take everything you have." I'm afraid we are heading in that direction unless the American people rise up to put a stop to it. Maybe there is hope, given the tempestuous nature of many recently-held "town hall" meetings throughout our country on the recent healthcare reforms by our politicians, the expansion of the "Tea Party" movement (which, although I support its basic beliefs, has its own radical right component), and the election of Senator Scott Brown (Republican) of Massachusetts, one of the most liberal states in our country, to occupy the seat vacated by the death of Senator Ted Kennedy. The majority of Americans are angry, and, although the Social Democratic Party (the Democratic Party that stood for the working class no longer exists), has won a major piece of legislation, I am very suspicious of its benefits and very concerned about the burden it will place on our country.

ABORTION

The abortion debate exploded on January 22, 1973, with the U.S. Supreme Court decision in Roe vs. Wade. In that decision, the Court held that a woman may abort a pregnancy for any reason until the fetus becomes viable (able to survive outside the mother's womb) — determined to be about 24-28 weeks. The Court further concluded that if a mother's life is in danger, a pregnancy can be terminated at any time. This debate continues in full force today as undoubtedly one of the most controversial, emotional, and politically charged issues ever decided by the Court. The issue stems from the right to privacy and the due process/equal protection provision of the 14th Amendment to our Constitution, which, among other things, protects the individual from undue interference from the States.

In my view, this is one of the most divisive issues our country has faced (similar to "slavery" which caused the Civil War). It is so divisive that I suspect you, my children, will find areas of disagreement from me as I give you my opinion on the matter. First of all, there are those who believe my opinion has no legitimacy since I am not a female, and thus incapable of understanding the issue. However, I believe I am able to study and draw my own conclusions based on factors that do affect me and the society in which I live. So here they are:

- If a fetus is allowed to complete the entire gestation period, it will be a human being. Therefore, to arbitrarily stop its completion without sufficient reason is wrong and, in my view, tantamount to murder.

- There are sufficient reasons to terminate a pregnancy. The rationale for these reasons is based on the greater good for the mother and with little harm to society as a whole. In each of these cases, verification by competent authority is required, and, unless verification is accomplished, the pregnancy must continue.

The reasons are:
- If the mother's health or life is in danger.

- If the fetus is determined to be sufficiently abnormal so as to either not survive or to be born seriously handicapped so as to be unable to live a physically or mentally productive life.

- If the mother is impregnated by rape or incest. In these cases, the fetus must be aborted no later than a reasonable time (say one week) after pregnancy is verified.

The societal argument focuses on two sides: pro-life and pro-choice. I do not believe these are appropriate comparisons because they are not opposites. To explain, "pro-life" is fairly straight-forward. A pro-life believer wants the pregnancy to terminate with birth. A pro-choice believer wants the mother to freely choose whether to terminate the pregnancy. However, I believe the choice is made when a woman voluntarily chooses to have sexual intercourse without appropriate protections or contraceptives by either party. To allow the termination of a pregnancy only because a mother no longer cares to carry the child is not an option. Unless any of the above applies, the child's right to life is equal to the mother's right to life and society has an obligation to protect it. For society to allow abortion for any reason within proscribed times violates the unborn fetus's constitutional right to life and to the due process/equal protection provision of the 14th amendment.

I believe my position is the only correct position for these reasons:
- It is based on logical reasoning and not any religious belief or commandment (although the religious would no doubt interject the Commandment, "Thou shall not kill", which I accept, but do not believe, is a persuasive societal argument).

- It is not based upon selfishness or greed, but rather it requires someone who freely chose to engage in a certain behavior to live with the consequences for the greater result (a child).
- For society to accept abortion on demand, even within proscribed time limits, makes it a legitimate medical procedure for which I, as a taxpaying member of society, am forced to financially contribute.
- At the time of conception, a fetus begins the process of developing into a human life and that cannot be logically disputed.
- Society can provide for some specific exceptions (as listed above) based on the well-being of the mother or fetus but not for the mother's convenience.

Irrespective of my position, the facts are clear. Since 1973, there have been over 50,000,000 abortions performed in the United States (according to the Alan Guttmacher Institute, which monitors abortions for Planned Parenthood, which is a major proponent and provider of abortions and receives Federal funds). That amounts to an average of about 1.4 million legalized abortions per year. In my view, that is a truly sad statistic; yet as usual, we have made a political issue out of it rather than a moral issue. We have an obligation to protect the sanctity of life, and these statistics show we are doing an abysmal job. How sad!

"Legalized murder?"

CIVIL RIGHTS

The civil rights movement in the United States has a long and tempestuous history. Our founders owned slaves but, even they knew there was something inherently wrong with owning them. Contrary to some beliefs, slavery was not instituted by our founders but had been a standard practice carried over from Great Britain for about 200 years. In fact, based in part on the efforts of the founders, from 1780 to 1804, the territories of Pennsylvania, Massachusetts, Connecticut, Rhode Island, New Hampshire, Vermont, New York, and New Jersey all abolished slavery. Ohio, Indiana, Illinois, Michigan, Wisconsin, and Iowa all prohibited slavery by virtue of a federal law signed by President George Washington.

That being said, the Southern States were obviously very much ingrained in practicing slavery. When Lincoln was sworn in as President in March, 1861, out of fear that the Republicans would control the government, the Southern States began seceding from the union. Of course we all know the disastrous Civil War began in 1861 over the slavery issue. On January 1, 1863, the Emancipation Proclamation went into effect, declaring that all slaves in the Confederate States were free. The war ended on April 9, 1863, when Lee surrendered to Grant (Lincoln was assassinated five days later by John Wilkes Booth, who hated everything Lincoln stood for). With this history as a background, suffice it to say that the South was reluctant to change and until very recently, did not accept Negroes (African Americans as they are now called) into mainstream society.

As I mentioned in another chapter, racial prejudice was alive and living, even in the North from after the conclusion of the Civil War until my time. I will now skip ahead a couple of generations to the 1950s. Being raised in a Catholic Italian family, I had no interaction with blacks. There were none in my neighborhood, none in the public grade school I attended, very few, if any in the public junior high and none in the Jesuit high school I attended. In Tacoma, Washington, where I attended school, blacks were ghettoized in what had formally been the Italian ghetto, so they attended the schools on the South side of the City. My first interaction with them was in playing sports.

When I was a senior in College (1964), under President Johnson (interestingly, a Southern Democrat from Texas), the Civil Rights Act of 1964 was passed. The Act prohibited discrimination in employment, education, and housing, based on race, national origin, religion, and sex. In 1967, the Age Discrimination Act was passed prohibiting discrimination in employment of those between 40 and 70 years old. In 1990, The Americans with Disabilities Act was passed, requiring employers to "reasonably accommodate" those with disabilities.

Predictably, this created a new crop of attorneys, some to school and/or defend employers, others to file law suits on behalf of those allegedly damaged by discrimination. Of course, a new government agency was formed called the Equal Employment Opportunity Commission (EEOC), as well as a whole body of laws and new terms such as "disparate effect, disparate treatment, protected class, class action, affirmative action, etc."

Although these laws were instituted primarily because of discrimination against blacks, they also apply to many other minority groups. As a white (I arguably could be called Italian American, but no thanks; I am simply an American with Italian heritage), I felt considerable animosity towards the government coming up with the concept of "protected class". And to add salt to my wound they devised the concept of "affirmative action" that actually required employers and colleges to hire or admit a disproportionate number of minorities, even if they were less qualified (presumably, to speed up equalizing them in society to correct 200 plus years of inequality).

As a manager in the private sector, I was actually looking for very qualified minority employees to protect us from discrimination claims. My perception of the public sector (mainly government and universities) was completely different. Under affirmative action, they actually lowered their standards for minorities rather than providing greater enforcement of the equal opportunity rights already given them under our Constitution. As a consequence, many blacks (including black politicians and leaders) continue to use the "racism" card whenever they find themselves down and out and blame white society for their unfortunate plight. There is even a recent case of a former president using the "racism" card (the wise and omniscient Jimmy Carter).

As an example, Joe Wilson, a Republican member of the House from South Carolina, recently called President Obama a liar in an inappropriate outburst during the President's speech to a joint session of Congress. Although he apologized to the President, the Democratic-controlled Congress formally rebuked him for the outburst. That is purely political so I mention it only in passing to emphasize the point that Wilson has now been accused of racism. Among the accusers was our esteemed former president, Jimmy Carter, whose administration was the most inept in my life time. Given the tremendous progress made by many blacks through hard work, society continues to embrace the racism argument so I would expect blacks as a whole to continue to lack in the work ethic and entrepreneurial spirit that made our nation great.

Unfortunately, I believe the civil rights movement has resulted in an unintended consequence for many minorities, particularly blacks, in that Civil Rights protections have them believing that they will always be victims of racism. We only have to look at blacks as a sub-culture (crime, single mothers, etc.), to see the horrible result of government acting like their parent, and I have no clue where this is going! And the likes of Jesse Jackson and Al Sharpton have done a great disservice to the cause. Congratulations to Bill Cosby and his followers. They are doing more for blacks than our government could ever do.

"Peace be with you!"

GAY AND LESBIAN RIGHTS

Federal Civil Rights legislation for gays/lesbians has been virtually non-existent. Any legislation has been left to the States. Like abortion, this is a hot-button item, as it is for me. Simply put, males have penises, and females have vaginas and, like all mammalian species, they are biologically there for a reason. There are only three scenarios for those who don't see it that way or actually use these body parts in ways not intended:

- They choose not to
- They are genetically and/or emotionally ill
- They possess a combination of both

Regarding scenario one, although I find the choice obscene, I recognize their right to choose the gay life style (and use one partner's anus as a vagina, or use a finger or a dildo as a penis) as long as it causes no harm to anyone else. However, Society must not recognize these as legitimate life styles that deserve the same status as marriage because neither two males nor two females can copulate. To give those who choose this life style the same societal benefits as marriage is a travesty to the human species.

Regarding scenarios two and three, if one is ill, quite frankly, I am unsure how we should deal with this. It is certainly deviant behavior, but we all have a right to develop close relationships, and I will tolerate their so-called sexual orientation as long as they keep it in their bedrooms. As with scenario one, state-sanctioned marriage is not an option.

Many argue that homo-sexuality has been in existence throughout human history. This may be so, but the fact that it has been in existence since ancient times does not give any credence to making it a normal life style any more than the ancient existence of murderers and thieves makes their life style normal behavior.

I have known and worked with a few gays/lesbians in my life and I find them to be very likeable and competent in a social or business environment. They were also treated with the same respect as any other person. Thankfully, I haven't had to interact with any gay/lesbian who wears the lifestyle on his/her sleeve. I wouldn't take kindly to that. In that regard, as an ex-Naval Officer, we likely had some gays on our ships, but gays were not accepted by society at that time so it was never an issue. Today, with the new openness and attempt by the gay/lesbian movement to make it a legitimate and accepted life style, I am in full support of the, "Don't Ask, Don't Tell," policy instituted in the military by President Clinton, so the military can remain strong for our national defense, without such a major social distraction.

Our current President (Obama) has been very supportive of hate crime legislation and including gay/lesbians as protected under civil rights laws (a problem because of the ramifications beyond pure civil rights protection), but it is less clear whether he supports legislation to legitimize their right to state-sanctioned marriage. He does want to eliminate the military policy (I'm not ok with this). The marriage issue will likely end up before the U.S. Supreme Court and who knows what it will do (as of this writing, presumably under orders from Obama, Defense Secretary Gates relaxed the "Don't Ask, Don't Tell" policy in the military. Congress has subsequently repealed it).

"Gay pride?"

THE MEDIA

I have included the media discussion in this section because of its ability to influence political outcomes. There is no question the media is biased. This is not a new phenomenon; it has existed since the media became a viable entity during the early 1900s. Prior to that time newspapers were the only real source of news and they generally reflected the opinions of the publisher. The practice of "yellow journalism" was pervasive, that is, trumping up headlines and stories, using sensationalism to increase circulation.

When I was growing up, I paid little attention to the news. When television was introduced into our household in the early 1950s, the news was generally about a 15 minute segment on local news followed by 15 minutes of national news, provided to us by NBC, ABC, CBS (or the Mutual Broadcasting System that no longer exists). To me, it was boring.

Today, I have lost my confidence in journalism as a whole. And most in my circles have as well. Admittedly, my fiscal and social philosophy is right of center so I view most of the newspapers and television news with a great deal of suspicion. There are so many sources of news that one has to almost compare notes with each source to determine what is factual, if any.

Studies have been conducted since the 1980s and they have determined that the vast majority of journalists favor the Democratic Party, and thus, their personal bias is either purposely or inadvertently interjected (2002 study conducted by Dartmouth College, showed a large liberal bias in all major news outlets). Other studies have showed a strong liberal bias on such hot-button issues like abortion, affirmative action and gay rights. In addition, the media is controlled by very few people and/or organizations. The so-called mainstream media is largely controlled by Disney, CBS Corporation, Time Warner and General Electric (recently, they sold NBC to Comcast). Therefore, any newsworthy subjects unfavorable to these organizations are likely to be downplayed. Rupert Murdock, the CEO of News Corporation, the parent of FOX News, is a known libertarian and has a strong influence on FOX. In addition, major advertisers can and do influence news reporting.

With this as background, I say FOX, conservative talk radio, and the advent of the Internet have evolved as a counter-balance to the left-biased of what is labeled the "main stream news". If they hadn't come to fruition, I hate to think of the even more egregious imbalance that would have permeated our waves with a deleterious impact on our society. Admittedly, because of the emphasis on "conservative" and "liberal", the great majority of Americans are left out of the debate. Because of what John Avalon calls "Wing Nuts" in his book of the same title, our society has become extremely polarized with the extremes playing a much greater role, both in the media and in politics in general. When I watch the news, which is not every day, I tune in mostly to local news and FOX, while occasionally watching NBC News (almost never ABC or CBS, more out of habit than anything else). Since retiring, I rarely listen to talk radio since I no longer commute. Unfortunately, the majority party of today, our current President, and the liberal/conservative ideologues who are receiving a greater political base, are causing further polarization with their respective agendas.

Today, we have a Democratic Party-controlled Congress, a liberal Democrat as President, and now I hear talk of re-introducing the fairness doctrine which would force conservative news to provide equal time for opposing views. What a crock that is. Given the left bias that already exists, forcing conservative stations to provide equal liberal time is nothing but a political ploy because of the obvious success of these groups. President Obama continues to show his immaturity by publically criticizing many individuals who frequent these networks such as Rush Limbaugh, Glen Beck, Sean Hannity, etc., all who are primarily entertainers who cater to the conservative cause. Here, he can learn from past Presidents who were successful because they focused on solving the issues of the day rather than give any credence to personal criticism.

So, my children, what's the conclusion here? I believe it is important to stay up on current events; but regard all news reporting with some suspicion regarding the actual facts, particularly if it's a hot-button subject or a political matter. And, since news covers a large part of prime time these days, it is important to pick out real news from mere fill, of which there is plenty. I would try to gather the important issues of the day and then move on to something else rather than hearing for the 15th straight night the newest clues on the mysteries surrounding the death of Anna Nicole Smith or Michael Jackson, or the trials and tribulations of Tiger Woods. And finally, draw your own conclusions. Remember, all news media tries largely to play to your emotions rather than simply report the facts, so learn to discern the difference between actual reporting vs. bias and fluff. Enough said.

Now, let's move on to my beliefs and philosophy regarding government based on my experience and opinions I have formed by virtue of this history.

PHILOSOPHY ON AMERICAN GOVERNMENT

At the beginning of this chapter I quoted the Declaration of Independence. When a public official or military member takes the oath of office, his or her only goal is "to protect and defend the Constitution of the United States from all enemies, foreign and domestic." This is the sole reason the Federal Government exists. Our forefathers planned it that way and left all other powers in the hands of the states.

Through the last 230 plus years of our Nation's history, this original intent has slowly changed through legislation, executive orders and court decisions. In my view, some of these changes were inevitable and necessary e.g. civil rights and anti-trust legislation to name two examples. However, to have any validity at all, new legislation must always be a clarification or enhancement of <u>an individual's</u> constitutional rights and nothing more.

Unfortunately, that has not been the case. For example, the Federal Government has continued to expand its powers by taking away those powers that were intended to be in the hands of the states; it has become involved in taxing its citizens beyond what was ever intended by our founders; it has become overly involved in our educational systems; it has created wars that are illegal (only Congress can declare war); and has passed environmental, welfare and entitlement legislation never even envisioned by our originators. In turn, it has passed tax codes to either pay for government growth or to redistribute wealth beyond merely equalizing the playing field, ostensibly, to create equal opportunity for all. Pathetically, it has partnered with the media to further erode our rights under the guise of "political correctness", e.g. liberal judges have severely harmed our Judeo-Christian foundation and its traditions by interpreting our constitution's separation of Church and State to mean Christmas should not be treated differently than any other religious holiday.

Our current leadership appears to be more inept than the previous administration. So far, our current President has shown how articulate he is, but he has totally missed the boat on what is of utmost importance to Americans. I submit healthcare and energy policy are of much less priority than reaching full employment again and fighting the War on Terror (President Obama refuses to use that label). He also appears overly in debt to special interest groups and is responding accordingly. That is not good leadership!

We once were a proud nation comprised of citizens from all walks of life who looked at the American flag with great patriotism and awe. I believe most of us who have or are contributing are still proud of our country, but can't stand how are government has passed onerous regulation stifling our competitive edge, and is continuing to further a socialist agenda. That means we need a grass roots effort to get rid of the bad apples and there are many in both parties although it seems the "new" Democratic Party of the last two decades or so is much more to blame for this socialistic trend, with implementation of Part D Medicare by a Republican Administration and Congress as the glaring exception. Term limits would help this immensely, but I doubt that Congress will impose this on itself. So we must figure out a way to impose it on them.

Former Arkansas governor, Mike Huckabee, and others have promoted the idea of a fair tax (consumption tax) to replace the existing outdated tax code. This has a lot of merit. It may be just the medicine that our economy needs to pull it out of the doldrums, put spending money in the hands of main stream America, and enable us to better compete in global markets. This will be true change; not the band aid-type change our current president seems to advocate, given his continued support of whatever health care amendments come out of Congress, which are merely add-ons to the current broken system. Admittedly, implementing a new tax code will be a tough sell since it is a total departure from the way we have done things since 1913. It will take real leadership and vertical politicking across all party lines to implement. I'm afraid that kind of leadership will likely have to wait for future administrations.

These things are not likely to change without a massive revolution. And, I believe one is absolutely necessary. I'm not advocating a violent overthrow of our government leaders, but a slow, methodical drive to take back our Country. In the past, I have been more interested in preaching "adaptation". I have always told you children to stay out of the system. If you get a traffic ticket, pay it; if you are taxed, pay the tax; if a law is passed, obey it. Up to now, this has been the only way to protect your individual right so the government will leave you alone.

However, one can carry this philosophy only so far. I have expanded on some of the issues that should give us all pause and maybe stir us to legitimate action. In summary, here is my conclusion on the status of our federal government:

- It is too big.

- It has over-regulated business so that legitimate endeavors are too costly and time-consuming forcing business to relocate to foreign nations or allowing China, India (and others) to overtake our competitive edge.

- Under both Democrat and Republican Presidents and Congress, it has caused out of control spending.

- Politicians in general care less about the American people although they keep quoting the term in their speeches. They only care about being re-elected.

- It has expanded its power far beyond that ever contemplated by our founders.

- It is trending towards socialism and will continue that trend with the help of the liberals and hippies of the 60s and 70s who are now in the power structure.

- Both parties must share the blame, but they will continue to point fingers at each other.
- It will take a significant event (similar to 9/11, except it must be a constant day-to-day threat) to unite the country and it will need to be catastrophic in nature. No leader will likely evolve that will unite us until the threat is there. It must be a real threat and not one trumped up just to create fear.

It is time to take a close look at our nation. Its principles are dissolving before our very eyes. Here are my conclusions on how to bring us back:

- Analyze the voting records of the politicians and vote those who don't adhere to the basic principles of our founders out of office (I like voting for the candidate who I believe will do the least damage).
- Create a system where brilliant, but ordinary Americans with great resumes can be elected to higher offices without having to raise millions of dollars (England?).
- Limit the terms of members of senate to two terms and the house to four terms.
- We were founded on a belief in God and it's time to re-emphasize that belief. Individuals are free to believe what they want (and I do—see section on religion), but "In God We Trust" must remain. Irrespective of personal belief, these Judeo-Christian principles have served well as the backbone of our Nation.
- Equality means the right to life, liberty and the pursuit of happiness; not preferential treatment for anyone because of their heritage, skin color or belief. Get rid of laws such as affirmative action that promote this treatment and punish any institution that practices it.

- Restore emphasis on the sanctity of life. It is ludicrous to conclude that the unborn are not growing human beings and, therefore, with extremely rare exception, have a right to be born.

- Place the highest priority on protecting our citizens from terrorism and foreign enemies. Put the administration of the vast majority of social issues in the hands of the states. That means downsizing many agencies such as the Environmental Protection Agency, the Department of Fish and Wildlife, the Department of Education, and completely reorganizing and shrinking the Department of Health and Human Services, to name a few.

- Modify burdensome regulation such as the Endangered Species Act, the recently passed "Obamacare", and the federal tax code among others, so we can begin to compete with foreign nations once again.

- Do not tax the successful to transfer their wealth to the unsuccessful. Other nations have tried this and it resulted in their demise (see below regarding fair tax).

- The Federal Government has grown to a considerable extent to provide jobs for minorities. It's time for the private sector to provide those jobs, and develop programs so they are completely qualified.

- Throw out the existing tax code in its entirety and replace it with either a fair consumption tax on goods and services (15% ?), excluding food, or substantially simplify the current code by using a flat tax with two rates. Although I much prefer the former, in either case, the wealthy will pay higher taxes. Balance the budget with the revenue produced.

- Jump-start the economy by extending the Bush tax cuts and lowering both the corporate tax rate and the payroll tax.

- No additional entitlement programs. Phase out social security and create a safety pool for those in need from the general fund; distribute the funds to the states and have them administer it.
- Pass a balanced budget amendment to create a fiscally responsible federal government (a vast departure from what we now have).
- Promote legalized immigration and deport illegal immigrants, unless they are able to satisfy citizenship requirements. A citizen must be able to read and write English. Drastically minimize the use of Spanish or any other foreign language in official government or corporate documents.

We are still free to disagree, we have made great strides in the civil rights area, and we still have the strongest economy that drives the rest of the world. We can celebrate our strengths but we must strengthen our resolve to hold our politician's feet to the fire or we risk totally losing our way. That means that they are not liars, what they say, they will do; what they do is always in the best interest of our country and not for them personally or their political party, and they will focus on true solutions to legitimate issues/crises rather than promote fear to control the electorate or to move forward on their personal agenda.

I single out the following presidents in my life as individuals who did not adhere to these principles: Lyndon Johnson, Richard Nixon, Jimmy Carter, and Bill Clinton. Under the leadership of these presidents, our Country became further divided along ideology. I remain neutral on Franklin Roosevelt, JFK, George H.W. Bush and George W. Bush; history has or will label them. So far, our current President has the worst track record of any of them (compare his campaign promises with his actions) and, I predict, will be noted as the greatest deceiver of all, unless he moves to the right after the mid-term elections and modifies fiscal policy substantially to focus on private sector jobs.

Whether you agreed with them or not, in my life time there have been only three Presidents that have adhered to the principles of honesty and straight talk and action approach: Harry Truman, Dwight Eisenhower and Ronald Reagan. All understood the very limited role of the Federal government to "protect our nation against all enemies, foreign and domestic". They understood the value of dissent and promoted open discussion rather than further polarizing our Nation.

With that, I conclude my treatise on our government and our political system. I leave the future of our Country in your hands.

"Good luck!'

LETTER THREE: TO MY CHILDREN

"The most important things in life are your friends, family, health, good humor, and a positive attitude towards life. If you have these then you have everything!"

Author unknown
How poor are we?

"The mass of men live lives of quiet desperation. What is called resignation is confirmed desperation. A stereotyped but unconscious despair is concealed even under what are called the games and amusements of mankind. But it is a characteristic of wisdom not to do desperate things."

Henry David Thoreau
Walden

FRANK A. RUFFO JR.

HAPPINESS IS EARNED

Life is a journey lived one moment at a time. Our minds attach a past but we can only live the present and plan for the unknowns of the future. The person who does this successfully stands a better chance of achieving happiness.

So my children, this letter will focus on my experiences and my relationships from my earliest memories through my retirement, some eventful, most not; the few relationships that lasted and the many more that did not.

EARLY YEARS AND PRESCHOOL
(1942-1946)

Little Frankie at Sunset Beach Home

My first few years were pretty much a blur with a few exceptions. Before I was age five, we lived in an inexpensive home on North Prospect in Tacoma just off of Sixth Avenue (the dividing line between North and South Tacoma). This was my parent's second home. As an infant and toddler, I lived in a waterfront home on Sunset Beach in Tacoma, but my folks moved because the main railroad line from North to South ran through our backyard and I apparently wandered out there which scared my folks into moving elsewhere (I remember nothing about this home). Thus, they purchased the house on Prospect Street in about 1943 or '44.

Once in a while, Dad cooked breakfast on weekend mornings. It was always country scrambled eggs with cut bacon or ham and toast. He was not an accomplished chef, but it tasted good to me.

The house was always cold; it had an oil-fired stove in the living-dining room area and that was it. So there was an electric heater in the kitchen. One morning for some reason, I threw a plastic squirt gun into the heater and caused a large fire on the kitchen counter which Dad doused with a bucket of water. I don't remember being disciplined for it but those flames seemed awfully big to me.

My bedroom was upstairs. The stairs were painted a light gray and were very slippery. I slept in a room that had a cheap shade on the window. On a breezy night the tree outside my window would brush against it. I could also see the shadow of the moving branches through the window shade. All this scared me out of my wits.

I had a blue doll that protected me in those days. Her name was Tina and we were inseparable, particularly at night (interestingly, my daughter is named "Tina"; wouldn't Freud have a time with that). I was sure some goblin or something was going to come through my window. Anyway, I apparently lived through those traumatic nights since I can write about them today.

"Thank Tina doll for that!"

My brother, Gary, was born on February 14, 1946, while we still lived in the Prospect Street home (we were three years and nine months apart). The house was very modest, but Dad being a truck driver for Camarrano Brothers, it was the most he could afford so Gary slept in the bedroom with Mom and Dad.

GRADE SCHOOL
(1947-1954)

I started kindergarten at Grant Grade School in the fall of 1947. School was a half day. I was entered into the morning session and walked to and from school which was about four or five blocks. I had to walk by a house that had a cyclone-fenced side yard with a large German Sheppard dog that barked fiercely at me every day. This was unnerving to say the least, but the dog never got out so I learned to tolerate it.

Our kindergarten teacher's name was Mrs. Larson. She seemed awfully old to me. She was probably in her late twenties or early thirties. Anyway, we used to sit on a rug on the floor. There was a kid name Billy Boyd (I always thought he was related to William Boyd, i.e. Hopalong Cassidy, a popular movie cowboy of that day) in our class. One time, Billy was sitting Indian style right in front of me and a switch blade knife with a beautiful handle started falling out of his back pocket. Billy had showed me this knife a short time before and I was very envious of it. So I leaned forward and stole the knife. Out of guilt, within the week I returned the knife and told Billy that I found it and knew that it was his.

"Bravo! I successfully completed my first moral lesson."

The first through sixth grades were also at the old Grant Grade School. I remember every one of my teacher's names (in order: Mrs. Larson, Mrs. Egan, Mrs. Heft, Mrs. Jones, Mrs. Norton –married during the year and became Mrs. Beafeaux, Miss Schuster; and Mr. Knutson). The school building was a very old three story structure with the third story condemned and used only for storage. We were all sure that there were ghosts on the third story since we were prohibited from going up there.

Grant Grade School was about three blocks from our Prospect home and about six blocks away from our new home on Cedar

Street. We walked to and from school (there were no school buses). I was a good student and liked all my teachers except Mrs. Schuster (fifth grade). I remember her writing on one of my report cards, "We must try to be calmer." My years at Grant (Kindergarten through sixth grade) were uneventful except that this was during the era of the Soviet Union and there was a high concern of them using nuclear weapons against the United States; so we saw a lot of films on what to expect in the event of a nuclear attack and how to prepare for it.

By the end of my kindergarten year, we had moved into the house my folks had built at 948 North Cedar. This was a beautiful home and my mother was very proud of it. Dad had left his delivery-truck job at Cammarano Brothers and entered into a 50/50 partnership in General Beer Distributing Company which distributed the local beer of the day, Heidelberg. Heidelberg was brewed in Tacoma and, at the time, was the number one seller in Pierce County, where we lived.

Dad made more money than he ever imagined, and thus, was able to build the Cedar street home. I don't remember the cost of the house, but it was a tidy sum for those days. As was customary for most folks at the time, Dad paid cash for the house. Shortly after moving into our new house, mother became pregnant, much to her surprise. Since they already had two boys, they were hoping for a girl, but on November 26, 1950, she gave birth to her third son, my brother, Dan.

During my first grade year, Mom decided I should take accordion lessons. She enrolled me with several other Italian boys in weekly lessons with Louie Nomellini, the local accordionist who taught many boys of Mediterranean heritage. The accordion was very popular in those days; we were required to participate in several accordion recitals. I started with a 12 bass accordion (the number indicates the number of bass keys played by the left hand; graduated to an 80 bass, and ultimately, a 120 bass, the largest made).

Holidays were fun. They were all celebrated with Mom's side of the family. Easter was at Aunt Barbara's; Fourth of July was at our beach house; Thanksgiving was at our town house; Christmas Eve, at Aunt Barbara's; and Christmas Day at Nana Helen's. Even the menu was standard. Easter, Nana Jenny's ravioli (one of my favorites); 4th of July, pot luck; Thanksgiving, traditional turkey dinner (Mom was a pro at this); Christmas Eve, pesto pasta (another favorite, meat was forbidden); Christmas Day, spaghetti and meatballs (polpette). Fortunately, all three ladies were outstanding cooks. These meals, coupled with all the traditional Italian goodies (scalili, kinolili, turdille, ginette, mustastole, frizini), made good Italian food a lifelong love. I learned how to cook many of these to carry with me for life.

These years were particularly memorable. During the school year living in our Cedar Street home, our neighborhood was filled with kids to play with. There was Dave and Don Peterson, who lived across the alley, Paul Benefield, next door, Don Munson, Harry Adams, Larry and Roger Ord (later Don Williams' family moved there), Jim Ball, and Ted Lundquist (and Pam Price, Peggy Gladstone, the two gals who lived close by). We played a lot of street football; Dad had put a basketball hoop over our garage and we would play horse or two on two or three on three into the dark (darkness was 4:30 PM in the dead of winter).

We also played baseball. In a game on our front street, while I was acting as catcher, a kid name Ford swung and on his back swing, the bat hit me above my right eye causing lots of bleeding and requiring stitches. Dr. Brooks, our family doctor, made a house call to repair my wound, and I, screamed and hollered to the point where there was no way he could stitch it up so he bandaged it as best he could. It healed and I still have a small scar above my eye to this day.

Me in about 5th or 6th grade   *The Cedar Street Gang*

JUNIOR HIGH SCHOOL
(1954-1956)

After the 6th grade, I entered the 7th grade at Jason Lee Junior high School. As I did in grade school, I almost always walked to Jason Lee which was about 14 blocks away. Although there were Tacoma buses that traveled their regular routes, there were no District buses for Jason Lee, at least as I remember. I would occasionally take the 6th Avenue bus partially home but the bus stop was still about four to five blocks from our house.

It was at Jason Lee where I started noticing girls. Jason Lee was a very cliquish school. It was 1954 and rock and roll was entering the music scene big time. The "in guys" wore black tee shirts under an open collar pink shirt, white pegged denims with a thin suede belt, with buckle on the side, and wedge shoes. Jackets were white, pink, or black stag worn open with collar up and leather jackets in winter months. We also had long hair greased down and combed in a duck tail.

Of course, wanting to be part of the crowd, I talked my mother into all the right garb. Even so, I never was part of the "in group" because of the values they promoted. These were: defy authority, get in fights after school, be belligerent in school, and generally be hoodlums. The "in girls" of that day seemed to really buy into guys like this.

However, I was not a saint myself. One night about 10 o'clock, we were walking home from downtown Tacoma. There were three of us and we walked through Wright Park, a fairly good sized park that had a care taker, with his wife, living in a house located on the Park grounds. We started throwing rocks at his windows, and, of course, attracted all kinds of attention. The caretaker called the police and shortly thereafter, we found ourselves hiding from their spot lights and flash lights. All three of us split in different directions. I jumped into a bush filled with thorns and a cop on foot pointed his flashlight right around me, but didn't see me. After he left, when I thought the coast was clear, I walked home alone. That was the last time I did anything so immature (and stupid) until high school.

It was about this time that I started playing little league baseball and football. Playing sports gave me the opportunity to give up accordion lessons even though Mom and Dad had just bought me a new 120 bass Sonola. I quit playing much to Mom's disappointment (and ultimately mine as well; I have taken it up again in my retirement years and give pause to how much better I would be today if I had continued the lessons).

THE BEACH

Shortly after completing the Cedar Street home, Dad and Mom started looking for a summer home on the Peninsula. Since it was in 1948, there was no Narrows Bridge (the original bridge only lasted 6 months, from July 1940 to November, 1940, and blew down in a single day-November 8, 1940). I'm guessing one of the reasons this made sense to them was there was another Narrows Bridge under construction and it was scheduled to open in July 1950.

Anyway, at that time, the mode of transportation was by ferry. We made several boat trips from Day Island to Point Fosdick. We first looked at a place on Horsehead Bay, but finally settled on a wonderful piece of property in a place with several acres called Moorelands named after McAllister and Alice Moore, the original owners, who sub-divided the acreage into many parcels. The Moores still resided on the upper side of the acreage, about a quarter of a mile from our property.

This property was a paradise. It was heavily wooded with high bank on the Carr Inlet side facing McNeil Island (although someone had bulldozed about a 30 foot cut at the center of the property to make it low bank (about six feet). The main cabin was one room and faced Shaw's Cove on the backside of the property. Since the property was heavily wooded, there was only a bulldozer trail leading to the cut facing McNeil. Both sides of the property were woods which isolated it from other cabins/homes. On the east side was a sand spit with an old liberty ship on it apparently purposely grounded to preserve the spit. What a playground the spit and the old ship would turn out to be for us kids.

Over the next few years, Dad and Mom totally reshaped the property. Since the upper side (facing McNeil Island had by far the best view, they purchased the parcel immediately west of theirs, they hired the only contractor on the Peninsula at the time (Spadoni Brothers) to shove the rest of the high bank into the bay for both parcels to ultimately create two low bank waterfront parcels of 120 front feet and 100 front feet.

After clearing the first parcel, they moved the cabin from the Shaw's Cove side to the Carr Inlet side, and expanded the cabin into a three bedroom beach house with a covered patio and a carport (could anyone even imagine the environmentalist uproar that would be in play today — it could never be done [see the Environmental section in the chapter on government]).

Our first summer actually living there was in 1951, the summer after the opening of the second Narrows Bridge. I was nine years old; my brother, Gary, was five and brother Dan was one and a half. Every summer since then we moved to the beach on Memorial Day weekend and moved back to our town house in Tacoma on Labor Day weekend.

Because we lived on the water, I fell in love with boats. My second cousins, Joe and Richard Carbone, had a 12 foot speed boat with a 15 horse Evinrude outboard motor. I pushed Dad for a similar boat. During our third summer (1953), Dad did purchase a 10 foot pram that had a little steering wheel attached to the middle seat. He already owned a three horsepower Evinrude from our 14 ft. row boat (which Dad named FRAGADA, i.e. for Frank, Gary, Danny) that he put on my pram. It was a letdown from my expectation in that its maximum speed was about 10 knots, but I was glad to have it and used it for two summers.

The following summer (1955), Dad purchased the speedboat from the Carbones, which was a joy for me. I used that boat for one season until it became obvious that due to the pounding the boat took over the years (it constantly bounced when on a plane), the bottom was separating from the frame. We sold it.

It was about this time (summer, 1956) that our family met Joe and Pat Cowan. Joe was an excellent boat builder of outboard racing boats and runabouts. I became intensely interested in boat racing, given this period was also the heyday of hydroplane racing in Seattle. Joe had built a Class C/D Utility racing boat, which he wanted to sell to build another for himself. Towards the end of the summer, Dad bought it for me with a 30 horse Johnson outboard Cowan had on it for power. We launched the boat in the Cove (Shaw's Cove, behind our home), in the evening in the presence of many friends and relatives, including Joe Cowan. I couldn't start the motor so, out of frustration, I locked the crash throttle at full speed forward gear. I stood up to start the motor by pulling on the pull cord. The motor started, the bow went up in the air and I came close to falling out of the boat. However I fell against the motor which kept me in the boat and I regained control of it. What a show I put on for the audience, along with a good ass-chewing from Cowan!

Over that winter the Johnson outboard froze up and became irreparable so Dad bought me a new Mercury Mark 30 which qualified me to race in CU Class runabout. I spent the next two summers in that boat. During those summers, I raced in the Vashon Island and Fox Island Marathons; I didn't finish either race, the Vashon Island because I didn't properly pre-launch the boat and test the carburetor adjustments that had moved out of place during the transportation to the pits. Regarding, the Fox Island Marathon, I followed Joe's lead and commenced a flying start under the Narrows Bridge and timing crossing the starting line in front of TOA (Tacoma Outboard Association) launch as the clock hit 0 and the starting gun went off. The Mark 30 was cavitating due to turbulent waters caused by the massive number of boats participating in the race. By the time I turned the corner and headed up Hale's Pass, the motor started to overheat and actually caught on fire under the Fox Island Bridge. I needed to be towed back to the pits.

As crew chief, Dad had had enough! He didn't want to participate in any more races because it was physically hard on him. I agreed so we quit. That ended my formal racing career, although I used the boat recreationally through the summers of '57 and '58.

HIGH SCHOOL YEARS
(1956-1960)

My high school graduation, May 1960

In Letter #1, I talk about my introduction to Bellarmine, and my first days there. Suffice it to say, after my public school experience, Bellarmine was a real challenge. The Jesuits piled home work on us like I hadn't experienced. There were evenings when I had six to seven hours of homework study. I remember sitting at my bedroom desk with all my school books completely frustrated as to how I was going to complete all my assignments. I studied exceptionally hard my freshman year and, as a result, I ended up with a 4.0 average.

As a new comer to Bellarmine, I developed a strong sense of competitive spirit which is what the Jesuits desired. All classes and activities were organized by your contribution; that is the best in each area got to be on the top rung. For example, freshman classrooms were alphabetized A through D. Students were placed in each class based on a combination of intermediate school grades and scores on the school's entrance exam. A and B classes were comprised of essentially the same caliber of student. In both classes, students were highly competitive. I was placed in B class with my friend, Gene Pentimonti.

Participation in outside activities was strongly encouraged. Since I transferred from a public school, I was too late to sign up for the frosh/soph football team. Although disappointed, I did participate in freshman elocution, the debate club, the Sodality (A religious society with special devotion to Mother Mary), freshman basketball, and baseball and became a class officer.

My sophomore year, I became a bit of a class cut-up. Bellarmine, being an all-boys school in those days, gave rise to more of this type of behavior. As a result, my grades began to suffer a little, although I still ended the year with a 3.6. At Bellarmine, the teachers rotated classrooms rather than the students (except for classes requiring a lab, a specialized piece of equipment or physical exercise). We each had our own desk for all classes so you could leave your materials in the desk bins. The bins were closed off unless you lifted the desk top, except for a hole called an ink well. I sat in the far left row adjacent to the windows about five seats back.

Anyway, there was an empty desk in front of me so I thought it would be cool to use it for something. So secretly over several days we collected a combination of dirt, weeds, etc. to build a nice pen for two to three garter snakes. We collected the snakes, put them in the pen and fed them with worms and bugs as we could. This went on for a couple of weeks until one of the snakes began to crawl out of the ink well. Since this occurred in the middle of Fr. Seipp's (then a scholastic, a student not yet ordained) Latin class, there was nothing I could do to remedy the situation without getting caught. The snake became a major distraction and everyone in the class started giggling. Fr. Seipp, who noticed the unusual happenings at the desk, walked over to it, lifted the top and observed our man-made snake pit. He immediately stopped class and made me and a couple of others clean out the desk. I, of course, spent several nights after school in JUG (Chapter 1, Judgment under God) raking rocks.

Another memorable and "not so cool" event occurred in history class. Fr. Michael Walsh, who was also then a scholastic, taught us history. One day before he entered the classroom, we spread a bunch of B-B's on the floor. When he entered the room, he did slip but (thankfully) didn't fall. Needless to say he was very upset, but no one would spill the beans so they never did find out who did it (I was involved along with several others). The punishment was several extra homework assignments for the entire class.

These antics are descriptive of my sophomore year. I did continue to participate in several extracurricular activities including sophomore football, basketball, Sodality, and was re-elected a class officer. I specifically recall entering a couple of elocution contests. In these contests I did a piece from Shakespeare's Macbeth and a sermon given by a black Southern Baptist preacher. Actually I did quite well with these. These contests were in front of parents and students during the evening and I found I was not intimidated by being in front of large audiences which was to bode well for me in my future.

Unfortunately, I did not participate in baseball, the sport in which I had the most talent, which was to haunt me during the next two years of high school. I decided to participate in boat racing which became known by the coach. He did not take kindly to my decision as you will see. Anyway, that about summarizes my sophomore year, which ended up as pretty much a combination of me participating in several activities, exhibiting sophomoritis (which resulted in my share of nightly JUG), and struggling to maintain my grade point average.

Not so in my junior year. In June, after the completion of my infamous sophomore year, two things took place. First, I turned 16 years old which meant I could drive a car. Second, I had my first taste of falling for a girl. My father bought me a 1954 Chevrolet Bel Air hardtop. It was a sweet-looking car for its day (although gutless). The girl's name was Janice and she was my definition of a fox. I saw her for the first time at the annual Father's Day community pig roast that took place on the sand spit close to our beach house. She was a real knock out. She lived at Arletta, which was about a mile and a half from our place. I introduced myself to her and we hit it off. From that point on, she became my "summer love" for the summer of '58. I will always remember my Dad's remark when I brought Janice home: "Where did you find such a 'shapely' girl"?

Although we dated exclusively for the summer, there were two issues that came between us. One, she had recently broken up with a guy she had gone with for quite some time from the same school as she (and for whom she still cared for and ultimately married); two, since we lived in Tacoma during the winter, I was viewed as a "townie" and was, thus considered an outsider.

This became clear when we attended any Peninsula functions, as I had to be prepared to defend myself from both verbal and physical attack. On one occasion I actually got into a fight with a local kid outside the hall where a dance was held. We finally called it a draw, shook hands and went back inside. After that, I was more accepted as a member of the group.

On another occasion, Janice and I were riding in a station wagon filled with six of us. The driver was driving too fast for the country roads and he ultimately flipped the vehicle after failing to negotiate a curve. Two of the passengers were seriously hurt (one being the older sister of one of my good friends—Nancy Pentimonti). They were taken by ambulance to a hospital in Tacoma. The rest of us had minor cuts and bruises, but nothing serious. We were given a ride home by the Washington State Patrol. Thankfully, all recovered fully.

In September, we moved back into town and started another year of school. Although Janice and I met at the Puyallup Fair that September (she worked there), that was to be our last date. I returned to Bellarmine and she returned to Peninsula High and her ex-boyfriend.

My junior year at Bellarmine was to prove to be very interesting. I continued my participation in extracurricular activities including joining the Glee Club, the Lion's Club, and the Letterman's Club at the end of the school year (members were required to have a varsity letter). As in my sophomore year, I played football, but was not a starter. Although I liked football and our coach, Jack O'Loughlin, somehow I hadn't yet developed into the player I wanted to be. Therefore, I didn't get to play very much which was very demoralizing. Although I played once in a while, I was not awarded a varsity letter.

"Ah yes, another lesson in the fairness of life!"

At the end of football season, I decided not to play basketball since I felt I was not going to be a significant addition to the team. I joined the ski club which was a supposed no-no for basketball and baseball players. I had never skied before so I rented my equipment. In those days, the skis were still made of wood, were very long and narrow with very tight bindings.

Every weekend during the winter of '59, several of us ski club members went on Saturday or Sunday ski outings. My last ski outing was a trip with several ski club members to Paradise in Mt. Rainier National Park. The Park only had a rope tow, but the first part of the run was very steep. Anyway, several of the more accomplished skiers built a small ski jump on the steep part of the slope. I decided to try the jump and in doing so took a big spill resulting in a broken left ankle. I was carted off the mountain in a stretcher and spent the rest of the day in the back seat of a car with my ankle in a splint.

The ankle took months to heal and, although I started baseball practice in the spring, I could not perform up to par. I finally had to confront the fact that I couldn't play and, as a result, stayed on the team as equipment manager (for which I earned a varsity letter without having played one inning!). What I didn't know was the negative impact my absence from the baseball program my sophomore year plus the injury my junior year from the forbidden sport of skiing was to have on my baseball participation my senior year.

I had continued with some of my sophomoric antics during my junior year for which I found myself in the principal's or vice principal's office a couple of times. The last time I was there, I was warned by Fr. McDonnell that one more incident may result in my suspension from school. That caught my attention and I immediately straightened up. However, I became a victim of circumstances totally out of my control.

Our chemistry classroom was arranged with an aisle down the center and seats on each side of the aisle. The aisle had a large rubber mat covering it that was glued to the floor. I sat in the back seat next to the aisle and a classmate, Jim Schindler, sat across from me. Over time those students sitting on the aisle kept pulling the mat loose from the floor when the teacher, Fr. Lawlor (then a scholastic), was facing the chalk board. Because of my warning from Fr. McDonnell, I did not participate.

Finally, the mat came loose from the floor and when Fr. Lawlor was facing the board, Schindler grabbed the end of the carpet and caused it to roll towards the front of the classroom. Fr. Lawlor turned around and immediately said, "Ruffo, get out!" I was shocked and begged him not to do that since if Fr. McDonnell caught me in the hall, I would be suspended from school. That didn't matter to him so out I went.

I knew I couldn't stay in the hall without getting caught nor go in the restroom where guys were noted to hide by standing on a commode in a stall. Fr. McDonnell was on to this so that was one of the first places he looked. So I made the decision to leave the school grounds, which was forbidden during class. I drove around Point Defiance Park for several hours thinking this was going to cause considerable problems for me, embarrassment to my folks since my father was president of the men's club and my mother was president of the women's club. It was getting close to dinner so I decided to go home.

When I arrived home there were two Volkswagen Bugs parked in front of our home (driven by Bellarmine Jesuits). I knew it was time to face the music so I came in the back door of our house which entered the kitchen/family room. Seated at the kitchen table were my parents, Fr. Sneeringer, and Fr. McGuire. They held a serious discussion with me in which I was able to tell my whole side of the story. They made arrangements for me to meet with Fr. McDonnell the next morning.

Although I was very much afraid of the meeting and had a sleepless night, the next day I went in to meet with him. He told me that he would allow me back in school after I withstood some punishment. I said okay. He then took me in the gymnasium, locked all the doors, told me to grab my ankles and proceeded to beat me on the rear until I fell to the floor. I then was allowed back in school.

Back to the 1954 Chev. I loved the car! I had it lowered (springs cut) and the hood leaded (hood ornament removed). Owning my own vehicle gave me a lot of freedom. Unfortunately, this freedom resulted in much less attention to my studies and I ended up my junior year with an abysmal 2.2 grade point average for the year. So much for my junior year. My senior year was to be much different and my most positive year since I was a freshman (with baseball being the sole exception).

But before we leap into my senior year, I must talk about the summer of '59. As usual, on Memorial Day, we moved to the beach and I went to work for the Pierce County road gang as a laborer. I didn't know it at the time but I was to meet a gal that summer who would be a major part of my life for several years. Her name was Pam and her parents had a summer place on the inside of Horsehead Bay which was very close to our beach house.

I met her totally by accident. I was visiting a summer friend of mine, Don, who happened to live next door to Pam. It was a warm day during June and since both houses were on the water we had an open view of the neighboring yards and docks. Pam was parading in front of her house in a pretty white bathing suit. I found her very attractive and eventually we started talking from afar. Pretty soon we went over to her place and thus began a relationship that was to last almost six years.

Life was good then; there were those who, on observation, would likely say we lived in a charmed bubble and I wouldn't argue with them. Simply put, I was fortunate to be in this environment. Anyway, this was a great summer, working on the County road gang during the day and being with Pam, the Pentimonti's and other beach friends boating, fishing, water skiing and generally enjoying a carefree life.

Fall of 1959 brought my senior year of high school. Pam started her junior year at Clover Park High School in Lakewood, but we were both "in love" with each other so we talked almost every day (on black single land line home phones, which was all that technology offered then) and spent weekends hanging out. The "bubble life" continued.

Football season also was under way and this was to be my best season. I started all games either on offense or defense and ended playing offensive end, defensive end or offensive guard or defensive nose tackle. I always considered myself a tight end, but once I experienced playing defensive nose tackle, I found I enjoyed that position because of the ability to be involved in lots of tackles as well as sacking the quarterback. Anyway, prior to the last game of the season against Lincoln High School, I suffered a severe hip pointer, but still played as much as I could. The season's results were we won the Grid-Go-Round (four Tacoma high schools played each other for one quarter to start off the season), won five games and lost three. I ended up making the second team all Northwest Catholic as a guard—primarily because of my play against O'Dea where I sacked the quarterback several times. This season was to be my soul glory on the grid iron; for, I never donned a football uniform again (although I was a starting end on a flag team in the Navy during the fall of 1965)!

During the '59-'60 school year, I became involved in additional school activities, including President of the Sodality (see the chapter on religion regarding my conflicted religious life), the glee club again, joined the junior prom committee, and became co-editor of our high school annual, "The Cage", along with my good friend, Gene Pentimonti. During late winter, the school held a boxing "smoker" in which participants were supposed to box their opponent for three rounds. Having boxed quite a bit with my younger brother at home, I entered the smoker and was placed against classmate Mike O'Brien (recently deceased, a close friend of mine throughout my life). I threw a lucky punch and knocked Mike out in the first round.

Spring brought baseball season and this year I was in tip top shape. To my dismay, I ended up alternating with another player as a starter in the outfield. But that was not enough. During our final game against Wilson High School which was for the City championship, I started in the outfield. Our baseball coach, Marion Pericin, came up with one of the most idiotic ideas I've ever seen. Of course, it involved me. Pericin decided that I would play right field whenever there was a right-handed batter and I would trade with Al Prentice at left field whenever there was a left-handed batter. Obviously, he decided that I was the weaker of the two fielders so Al and I found ourselves changing fields several times during an inning depending on who was at bat. Although this was highly embarrassing to me personally, I got the last laugh; for, virtually all the fly balls came in my direction and I ended up making two miraculous catches—in one case saving a home run and in another, several runs. We won the game but I never liked Pericin and his antics here solidified my dislike.

Senior graduation was both happy and sad. Happy, because I graduated as an honor graduate (barely—thank you junior year!). Sad, because I was to part with so many close friends that I had made at Bellarmine. I had been accepted to attend the University of Washington, Seattle U, Gonzaga University, and Santa Clara

University. I opted for Santa Clara, primarily because my father and my two uncles went there and it was in California. Classmates who were attending with me were Marty Petrich, Mike Harrison, and Joe Gonyea (a close friend to this day).

Summer vacation of 1960 began with high school graduation festivities. I hosted those graduates with whom I hung out or I played sports with to a party at our beach place. Many of us stayed overnight sleeping on the sand spit next to our house. We had plenty of beer and generally became rowdy and, I'm sure disturbed the neighbors. Dad was uncharacteristically nervous since he would have been responsible for supplying the beer to 18 year olds. He watched our antics form the back of our property for a large part of the night, until we fell asleep (passed out).

The other major event was an all-night party chaperoned by several parents (mine included) at classmate and good friend, Joe Gonyea's grandfather's farm. It was a hoot and, of course, Pam attended with me.

The rest of the summer closely paralleled the previous summer with me working for the County road gang and continuing to date Pam and generally enjoy life.

Pam and I before senior prom-1960

COLLEGE YEARS
(1960-1964)

 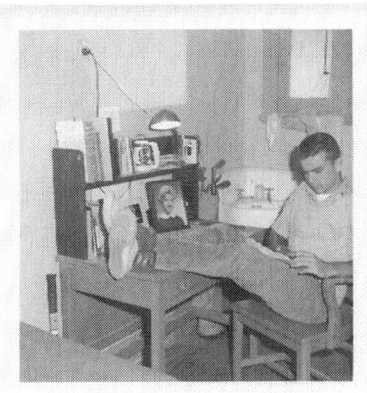

Santa Clara, O'Connor Hall freshman year, with Jim Hamm
Me studying at my desk

In September 1960, I prepared to leave for Santa Clara. During the summer, I had met Jack Ludwigson, my cousin, Joan Carnine's boyfriend, who would be starting his senior year there. Santa Clara had a rule that freshmen were prohibited from having cars. Since Jack lived in Bellingham, Washington, he offered to pick me up on his way south. On the appointed day in early September, Pam came to our house to see me off along with my parents and brothers. Jack arrived mid- morning in his Volkswagen bug; I said a tearful goodbye to all (especially Pam) and off we went to California.

Santa Clara was a whole new experience. We were pre-registered so the only real chore was moving in the dorm, meeting your roommate, and becoming familiar with the campus. I was assigned room 208 in O'Connor Hall, one of the oldest buildings on campus

(My father lived in the same building when he attended in the early '30s).

My roommate's name was Jim Hamm from Pacific Grove out on the Monterey Peninsula. Fortunately, we hit it off. I was a pre-med major as was Jim. I had elected that major during my senior year at Bellarmine based, in part, on two of my older cousins studying medicine and my Mom's desire for me to follow in their footsteps (no, she was not Jewish!). We had about four to five day's orientation and then classes started.

Although in those days, Santa Clara was known for both its basketball and baseball teams, they had resumed football after a hiatus of many years. Although I was tempted to turn out, I decided not to because of my heavy afternoon lab schedule. During the winter, I did start boxing but my Dad found out and asked that I quit. Since I was still a pre-med student, it didn't make much sense anyway so I let it pass. All in all, I had a mediocre year as a freshman at Santa Clara. We had a lot of fun but my grades averaged about 2.5 which were not up to speed to get me into med school. I was very homesick as was my buddy, Joe Gonyea. We both had girlfriends at home and we missed them immensely. Summer break finally came and we returned home. I returned to the county road gang for my third straight year and had another great summer at the beach with Pam and my old high school buddies.

One significant event that occurred that summer was Joe Gonyea's marriage to his high school sweet heart, Jo Mae Miller. Joe was quite a lady's man during his first few years of high school, and since he was 19 and Jo Mae was 18 I was unsure how long the marriage would remain stable. Nonetheless, they were married and I describe some of the specifics in the section on religion. Pam was in the wedding and I was Joe's best man (picture, page 23). It was quite an event, taking place in Mt. Vernon, Washington, (home of Jo Mae's parents) about 85 miles north of Tacoma. Anyway, after the wedding, Joe and Jo Mae moved to Santa Clara to find a place to live before the beginning of Joe's sophomore year.

I made the decision to return to Santa Clara, in part because I was hoping to improve my grade point average, and I didn't want to embarrass myself with my peers and folks. I felt I would fare better if I had a car in school so I talked Dad into footing half the cost for a white 1958 Chevrolet Impala convertible. This was a beautiful car, 348 tri-power engine with a three speed column stick shift ($1,800— I traded in my '54 Chevrolet for most of my half which Dad had bought for me in the first place!). So, once again, I said goodbye to Pam (who was starting her freshman year at Washington State) and drove my new car south with fellow class mate, Marty Petrich.

Upon arrival at Santa Clara, I moved into my assigned room in a much newer dormitory, Room 302 Walsh Hall, with Jim Hamm, my same roommate as my freshman year.

Sophomore year with the gang and my car in front of Walsh Hall

With the exception of my ability to frequent Joe and Jo Mae's apartment for dinner and camaraderie, my sophomore year showed no improvement from my freshman year, either in studying or sparking any interest in school activities. In truth, it was totally my fault. I spent most weekend time with my cousin, Jim (whose family lived in San Jose), messing around with cars and partying when I should have been hitting the books and becoming more involved in school activities, as I had done in high school.

In fact, I ended up spending many week nights and most weekends modifying my car with Jim's help by installing an aluminum flywheel, a stronger pressure plate for the clutch and a Hurst floor shift for the transmission. Unfortunately, when we installed the new equipment, we did not properly align the drive shaft or the transmission linkage, which caused the transmission to overheat and break. It was quite a sight seeing needle bearings all over the street. We towed the car to the service station down the block from my cousin's house (owned by a good friend of his family) and they fixed it properly.

By spring of my sophomore year I was fed up with Santa Clara. At the beginning of the school year, the University had gone co-ed (it was announced the year before) and that brought a cliquish atmosphere to the environment that had not existed my freshman year; there was the "in" crowd and the rest. Unfortunately, I became part of the rest and, although I know now that it was my own doing by not getting involved, I decided that I could obtain that same environment closer to home. So I discussed the matter with my folks and they reluctantly agreed to allow me to transfer to Seattle University. When I announced what I was going to do to my Tacoma class mates and my roommate, Jim Hamm, both Jim and Joe and Jo Mae Gonyea decided to transfer as well.

Santa Clara annual picture, 1962

The summer of '62 was different than the previous summers. I took a job with St. Regis Pulp and Paper Company in the Tacoma Tide Flats because it paid more money ($2.45 to $2.85/hr., depending on the job and shift). My first job was as a bailer, which was to mechanically pick up two compressed pulp bails at a time and place them on a conveyor belt to move them into the bailer. They would then be shipped to paper customers. This was hard work. It was also shift work. We rotated shifts every seven days. Our schedule was seven day shifts; two days off; seven swing shifts; two days off; seven graveyard shifts; four days off. We frequently were required to work either a half or full shift overtime (12 to 16 hour shifts), which, to some extent, was welcomed because it substantially increased our pay. If we worked a full double shift, the Company brought in a meal for us. We also were called in frequently to work on our days off. By the end of the summer, I made a point not to answer the phone unless I wanted to work a day off. As a requirement of the job, I had to join the Pulp, Sulfite, and Mineworkers Union and, of course, pay dues (little did I know then that in my career, I would be intimately involved with unions for many years).

Because of the hectic work schedule, I lived in our town home, which gave me a lot of freedom since the parents continued to spend summers at the beach with my brothers. I started frequenting my grandfather and grandmother's house (Papa Gus and Nana Helen) for meals, particularly breakfast. I would show up on a moment's notice and I was always welcome. Additionally, I frequently had friends over to our house for a little partying since we had a beautiful recreation room with a bar in the basement. Pam and I spent a lot of private time there as well, so, although the work at St. Regis was harder and much more involved, I liked the freedom of living alone.

That same summer, I was to meet Mike Hosterman, who would be a close friend the rest of my life. Mike had gone to O'Dea High School in Seattle and then matriculated at Portland University with John Egan, one of my high school friends, who introduced us. Mike and I hit it off immediately and we started hanging out together whenever time allowed. Mike will play an increasing role in my life, particularly after we begin our careers.

I have always had a love of the sea and war ships. Consequently, as a youth I dreamt of joining the Navy and becoming a Naval Officer. One night during the summer of 1962, myself and two of my high school buddies (Mike O'Brien and Jack Brady), visited the reserve submarine, "Cabazon", with Jack's boat. We came alongside the sub, knocked on the hull and the unlisted man on watch came topside and invited us aboard. He took us on a tour of the sub and I was totally enamored with it. We had some beer with us which we shared with him (since the sub was inactive, immobile and only used for training purposes, he was the only ship's company on board). Subsequently, we visited the sub two or three more times.

At the end of the summer, 1962, Pam returned to Washington State for her sophomore year and I started my junior year at Seattle University. Seattle U was on the quarter system rather than semester, so I lost some credits when I transferred which ultimately would require me to attend an extra quarter. I had made previous arrangements to room with my cousin, John Ruffo. Our room was in Bellarmine Hall, a brand new high rise dorm on campus.

Joining the Navy came about quite by accident. Shortly after commencing my junior year of college at Seattle University, Dad had met and sold beer to a Navy recruiter who was responsible for the Tacoma branch of the Naval Training Center (I believe he was either a Senior or Master Chief Petty Officer). One Sunday when I was home for the weekend, he invited the recruiter to dinner at our home. In addition to me, others present at the dinner were one of my high school buddies and college roommate, John Egan, and my brother, Gary (and, of course, my folks and little brother, Danny).

Before and after dinner, the recruiter talked to us about joining the Naval Reserve while we finished school. So we bit the bullet right there and signed up (me, Egan, and Gary, even though Gary was only 17 so Dad had to sign to okay his joining). We were enlisted in the Navy Submarine Division with the rate (rank) of Seaman Recruit and were required to report aboard the "Cabazon" one weekend a month for reserve duty with the understanding that we would serve two years active duty on an active submarine once we graduated from college.

While in college, one weekend each quarter, we traveled to Port Angeles, Washington by bus to go to sea with an active fleet boat (this was 1962-63 and the nuclear sub program was just getting underway). Fleet boats were diesel electric which meant the boats were propelled by diesel engines on the surface and with batteries when submerged and not snorkeling.

Anyway, life aboard a fleet boat could best be described as cramped and smelly. Diesel fuel smell permeated everything including our clothes and I suspect our skin. To compensate for the quarters, the food was outstanding and there was plenty of it. Unlike bigger Navy ships, the ship's officers ate from the general mess so all were served the same menu.

On submarines, there were two lookouts on the bridge when the boat was on the surface. Whenever the three blast signal was sounded indicating "dive, dive, dive", each lookout had the responsibility to jump onto the large front ladder leading to the coning tower and man the bow and stern planes to begin the downward angle of a dive. One weekend while practicing on an active submarine in the Straits of Juan de Fuca, Gary and I were lookouts and when the dive signal was sounded, Gary jumped to hit the larger step to scurry down the ladder. Unfortunately, he missed the step and plummeted down the ladder into the control room. Even though he had some bruises, he manned the stern planes and we submerged with me and Gary in control of the bow and stern planes.

At SU, I continued with my pre-med major. As part of the curriculum, I was required to take embryology. Our professor was a PhD Jesuit named Eugene Healy. I will always remember him because he was a terrible lecturer, gave no exams except the final, and he told us it would be one essay question. The question was something like, "Trace the various stages of a human embryo from conception to birth, diagramming, labeling, and explaining all phases of development." We were issued a blue book, which was a blank notebook about half the size of a regular sheet of paper. We were told there were more books on the desk and we had three hours to complete the work.

I worked feverishly for the entire time and, as I recall, completed two blue books. I placed them in the appropriate pile and left the classroom. Since the final was the only test we took, it was obvious the grade received on the test would be your final grade for the class. When my report card came, the grade was a "D" which infuriated me. To have the "D" on my grade report would make it impossible to get into any medical school so I paid a visit to Fr. Healy. The guy was a real SOB and could not come up with a good explanation for the grade. I left totally frustrated and made the supposition that Fr. Healy used his professorial power to arbitrarily determine who was "fit" for medical school and who was not. After that, I decided to change my major.

After having an in depth discussion with James Royce, S.J., the head of the psychology department, I decided to major in psychology starting winter quarter. This turned out to be an excellent move. I became extremely fascinated with the subject and studied it diligently. It would pay off as my grades were to drastically improve.

Winter quarter, I decided to move off campus. I moved into a three bedroom apartment called the Cherry Terrace with Jack Brady, a high school chum, and Paul Gustafson (Gus), who I knew from my summers in Gig Harbor. We only stayed there one quarter because we took the opportunity to move onto a large houseboat situated on Lake Union. Since it was so large, we were joined by John Egan, who transferred to the University of Washington from Portland U, and a guy named Stuart who was a friend of Jack's and ran a high fi shop in Bellevue.

This was good living. Although there was a lot of partying, I frequently stayed on the SU (Seattle U) campus to study in an empty classroom. With five of us living there, the rent was extremely cheap—$55 per month for rent and $50 per month for moorage split five ways! Jack, John and I took turns cooking and Jack and John started making sake in bulk, which was very good. Gus and Stu almost never ate there so it worked out fine.

Stu was a free spirit who regularly had sex with whoever, articulated a strong anti- government philosophy, and was a strong believer in Ayn Rand. Although he was not a precursor to the late '60s hippy movement, he was certainly different from the rest of us. He was very intelligent so I enjoyed having discussions with him. Like Stu, most students of the day were anti-government and Rand's philosophy of rugged individualism fit well with the college crowd. Her books, "The Fountainhead" and "Atlas Shrugged" were must reads for the college elite.

At the end of the school year, we decided to keep the houseboat throughout the summer of '63 since the rent was so cheap. Gus graduated at the end of spring quarter so Jack Fitzgerald, another high school friend, moved in after transferring from St. Martin's College to, presumably, the UW (I don't think he ever got in because of poor grades). Jack moved in during that summer while I moved back to Tacoma to take a new summer job at Carling Brewing Company (I had turned 21 and thanks to Dad, got the job). The brewery's bottle shop bottled for two shifts. I was one of four on the graveyard cleanup crew whose job it was to make the bottle shop spic and span for the day shift. This was a good job; we had a lot of freedom, it paid well, and, even though I had to pay dues to the Teamsters Union, it was well worth it.

Regarding naval reserve, during the summers we were required to spend two weeks on active duty for training. During the summer, Egan, me, and, my brother, Gary reported to Hunter's Point Naval Shipyard just outside of San Francisco. The training was rigorous and geared specifically to learning all the systems aboard a submarine.

However, most evenings were free so it gave us the opportunity to explore San Francisco, and explore we did. Even though I had gone to college less than 50 miles from the City (Santa Clara University my freshman and sophomore years), I had little opportunity to go to San Francisco, so we acted like drunken sailors (uniform and all), cruising Market Street, China Town, Fisherman's Wharf, North Beach. We were fortunate we made it back to the Training Center in one piece.

In the fall of 1963, I started my senior year at Seattle U and moved back onto the houseboat. Fall quarter of 1963 was personally memorable because of an event that would affect our country to this day—the assassination of President Kennedy. The details are in the section on politics, but suffice it to say, the age of tranquility was over and life in the United States was never to be the same.

Other than that, for me personally, this was a successful year. Pam had decided to transfer to the University of Puget Sound in Tacoma so we could be closer to each other so I went home every weekend to spend time with her. I was also doing extremely well in my studies with Psychology as my major. I excelled at statistics and was asked to tutor marginal students two evenings a week during winter quarter. I accepted and made a little extra spending money. Since I had joined the naval reserve, I continued with my duty of one weekend a month doing submarine duty either on the reserve submarine, "Cabazon", based in Tacoma, or on an active fleet boat out of Port Angeles, Washington.

During spring quarter, because of my transfer from Santa Clara and change of major, I learned I would not have enough credits to graduate and would have to complete one more quarter. I accepted that since it was unclear to me what I would do after graduation. I took the Graduate Record Exam (GRE) and the Law School Admissions Test (LSAT) and applied and took the test for Navy OCS. I also applied for a master's degree in Psychology at Columbia University and the University of Washington. Although I was accepted to graduate school, the Navy had other plans and denied me a deferment for post graduate work. Because of this and the fact I had done well in the test for OCS, by the end of spring quarter, I had decided to go to OCS in Newport Rhode Island after satisfying the requirements for a college degree.

The summer of 1964 would be both the same and different than the previous summer. The same in that I again went to work at Carling Brewery on the graveyard shift cleanup crew. Different, in that I decided to break up with Pam for reasons totally unrelated to her. Since I was going into the Navy after graduation, I felt it would be better if I was free from our relationship because I was going to be separated from her for a long period of time and, quite frankly, got cold feet regarding any marriage thoughts. Rather than confronting the issue with Pam directly, I took the easy way out and simply stopped contacting her which made it obvious to her that I was losing interest (a real coward). Anyway, that summer, I started dating Judy Bailey, a tall pretty gal that I had known of for many years, and, although our relationship was short-lived, we had a lot of fun together until I left for OCS in January 1965.

That summer, I also played baseball on a Gig Harbor industrial league team. One particular game is memorable. We traveled to McNeil Island Federal Penitentiary (it is now a State prison) to play the McNeil Islanders. It was a big event for the inmates. Virtually all of them (except the hardcore prisoners) were in the stands; they had a public address system that announced the players as they came to bat. The announcer announced, "Now batting, Frank Ruffo, left field." As I approached the batter's box, an inmate behind home plate yelled, "Hey Ruffo, hit one over the center field fence like your old man did (15 years earlier)." I lost my composure laughing and had to call time out before I could continue. I flied out to left center field.

Fall Quarter 1964, I moved into an apartment with Mike James, whom I knew at SU. He had graduated and started med school at the University of Washington. The apartment was close to the UW so I commuted to the SU campus daily. I graduated from college at the end of the quarter after being accepted to Naval Officer Candidate School (OCS) in Newport, Rhode Island. I successfully completed the requirements for Bachelor of Science Degree in psychology and received military orders to report to Newport, Rhode Island, to begin Officer Candidate School, the second week of January 1965.

CHRISTMAS BREAK
(1964)

This brief period was about to change our family's life forever. My brother, Gary, who had graduated from Bellarmine, started Gonzaga University fall quarter. Gonzaga had the same "no auto" regulation for Gary as a freshman as Santa Clara did for me. Since I knew I was going to OCS, I sold my car the previous summer and used Gary's car for my last quarter at SU (1964 Chevrolet Super

Sport four speed). On December 20, Gary flew home for Christmas break. I picked him up at the airport in his car and we drove home. The next day (December 21), we went to Seattle and bar hopped until late at night (Gary was18, but had no problem getting in bars). Since it was so late and my roommate had returned home to Alaska for the break, we ended up staying in the apartment. The next day (December 22), we returned home completely hung over and very tired.

That evening, we sat down for the family dinner and Gary was still very tired. He said he was going out with his girlfriend, Carolyn Kern, and doubling with one of his good friends, Jack Ancich, and his girlfriend, Lou Beckman. I was too tired to do anything so I retired early. About 11PM, mother awakened me in a panic and said Gary had been in an auto accident and was in "critical condition" in the emergency room at St. Joseph's Hospital. Then both of my parents left with little brother, Danny (then 14 years old). I quickly dressed and went to the hospital in the folks' second car. On the way, I suspected Gary was dead, and dreaded the thought of entering that hospital.

When I arrived through the emergency room doors, I heard Mom crying in a loud wail and saw Dad sobbing. Dad told me my brother was dead and brought me into the room where Gary was lying on a gurney, his body covered with a sheet. I threw back the sheet to see blood still exuding from his mouth. I covered him up and walked out into the hall way to see a Tacoma police officer lying on a stretcher with a cut lip. Dad told me that the officer was on his way to work and he hit Gary's car broadside while they were making a left turn. Gary died at the scene (I later found out from a broken neck). Although the others in the car were injured, all recovered.

I had a lot of sorrow and some guilt over Gary's death. I later found out he wasn't even driving his own car because he was too tired (from our all-nighter the night before). He was sitting on the right hand side of the back seat exactly in the spot of the impact and didn't have a chance. Since it was three days before Christmas, the folks decided to hold the funeral on December 29. For our family, it was truly the saddest Christmas I've ever experienced. In fact, since that Christmas, I've had misgivings about the season. (Mom, apparently very angry at God, did not go to Mass for at least 10 years after Gary's death). Over the years, I've softened a little because I do enjoy being around family and friends. Sandy, who is a wonderful cook, does a bang up job decorating our home, with little help from me. However, I do not participate in any religious aspects of Christmas nor do I relish the ever-growing commercialism.

Gary's funeral was attended by an overflow crowd at St. Patrick's Catholic Church in the north end of Tacoma with a very long funeral procession to the family plot at Calvary Cemetery. Who would have ever thought that he would be the first to be buried there?

Gary's 1964 high school graduation picture
Gary Ruffo Scholarship Outstanding Student Athlete award plaque

NAVY YEARS
(1965-1968)

Me, with family, leaving for OCS, January 1965

The next few days were a blur except I knew I was scheduled to report to Navy Officer Candidate School in Newport, Rhode Island on January 10, 1965. I debated whether to postpone leaving so I consulted with Fr. Sneeringer, who was close to Mom and Dad. He urged me to go as planned. "Get on with your life" he said, which I did. So on January 4, I left early for the East Coast with two other officer candidates who lived in Seattle and were assigned the same class. First stop, R and R in New York City, my first visit to "The Big Apple". We flew Northwest Airlines nonstop to JFK. The flight was memorable, to say the least. In those days, the airlines carried full fifths of liquor. We befriended the stewardesses (they were all young, gorgeous females as was the standard of the day—boy, do I miss that!). They poured us one drink after another and finally let us help ourselves at the back of the plane. All three of us got so drunk that during landing at JFK I was in the aisle crawling on the floor. If that happened today, they would have had me in handcuffs and carted me away upon landing.

After landing, we slept for a few hours at the airport before taxing it into the City. On the way in, I lost my traveler's checks in the cab. Coincidently, the cabbie's last name was Ruffo (a more common name on the East Coast) so I was very concerned about him cashing my checks. Since I had the traveler's check stubs in a different spot, I went to a bank and was able to have them replaced without much of a problem.

Between January 4 and January 9, we stayed in Manhattan. Our first night, we stayed at the downtown YMCA. What a trip that was! There were common bathrooms. While using the urinal, a "guy" next to me propositioned me, which was a major shock to me. I had heard of gays (we had various names for them in those days—homo, fag, fruitcake to name a few; the term "gay" had not yet been coined), but had never encountered one since it was taboo to be gay. Anyway, I told the other guys about the incident and we immediately moved to another hotel.

We did something New York-ish every night. We had heard about a new young comedian named Bill Cosby so we bought tickets to see a dinner show at "Basin Street East" where he was playing. He was hilarious and we all commented that he was going to move on to great things in his future (how right we were!). We also saw a young star named Barbara Streisand in a musical called "Funny Girl". She was great and we also thought she would rise to stardom someday (Once again, we were right, but I have long since lost all respect for her because of her arrogance and her social and political views). Lastly, we saw Sammy Davis Jr. in "Man with a Golden Arm".

On January 9, we bused it to Newport, Rhode Island, in preparation for reporting to OCS the next day. For the next three and a half years I became a member of the US military, which I relish to this day. While I was in OCS Training, I received orders to report to a fleet submarine in San Diego as an enlisted man. Because they were sent to my address of record (Tacoma, Washington), I wasn't aware of the orders until I learned that I was reported "absent without leave" while I was training at Newport. The Navy quickly fixed the records without further incident.

The first month at OCS was obnoxious. We were totally regimented between morning exercises upon reveille at 0530, meals in the mess hall, classes, evening study, and lights out at 2230 (10:30 PM). I survived it all and because of a combination of self-preservation, determination to be a leader, desire to excel, and my past enlisted experience. I became Company commander of our Company (Kilo Company) my "senior year" (fourth month), and was even a candidate for regimental commander of Class 509.

All candidates for regimental commander were interviewed by the "Board of Officers" before the green table prior to being selected. Strict military discipline was in order when appearing before the Board. As one entered, full attention to formality and squaring corners (turning at right angles) with appropriate salutes was a must when approaching the foot of the table. One had to visualize this—a whole cadre of senior officers occupying a long boardroom-style table with a green table cloth observing your every moment. The first question I was asked was, "Why do I want to be Regimental Commander?" I immediately responded with something like, "Because of my excellent military and leadership skills". This was a good answer but unfortunately for me, my Italian heritage came out, and while responding, I raised my right hand to gesture my response as well. Unfortunately this was not viewed as an appropriate act for a potential regimental commander so I was summarily dismissed, and had to settle for Company Commander. The successful Regimental Commander was Officer Candidate Hummel, of Juliet Company, our arch competitor. He suffered from short man's syndrome and I thought I was better than him even though I wasn't selected. I used to cringe as to why I raised my hand to make that gesture during the Board interview. Such is life as I was to find out big time later.

While at OCS and having been in the submarine reserve while in college, I explored the idea of joining the Navy's nuclear power program, which required a commitment of six years active duty rather than three, after the four month OCS training. I traveled to New London, Connecticut, which was the East Coast home of the nuclear fleet to explore that option. However, I decided to stay on the surface fleet with my original commitment, primarily because

Admiral Hyman Rickover, who was in charge of the nuclear program, personally interviewed all officers who were to potentially join the program and was noted as a real "asshole" in the interviews. Additionally, it required an extension of active duty for three more years when I hadn't made the decision to make a career of the Navy.

Officer Candidate School Class 509, Kilo Company (Me, fourth from left)

Officer Candidate Ruffo

Although there was obviously monstrous political fallout regarding our mission for those days, i.e. beating communism in Vietnam, we in the military in 1965 were committed to fighting to win the war. This was articulated by the instructors at Newport which made us young officers-to-be even more "gung-ho". So after graduating from OCS in May 1965 and awarded a commission as Ensign, I went to Mine Sweep School in Charleston, SC, having already received orders to the ocean minesweeper, "*USS Reaper*" (MSO 467), home ported in Long Beach, California, where I was to be stationed after graduating from Mine Sweep School.

Graduation from OCS, May 1965

Before leaving Charleston, and after graduating from Minesweeper School, my orders were changed to report to Naval Supply School for line officers, also in Charleston. So having to stay there for another period of time, my orders were changed from the "Reaper" to the "*USS Pluck* (MSO 464)", also home ported in Long Beach, where I reported in October 1965.

Prior to reporting aboard, I was awarded leave time and went home to Tacoma, Washington for R & R (rest and relaxation). While in Charleston, I started having low grade but consistent stomach pains so when I returned to Tacoma I visited our family doctor who sent me to a radiologist for a barium x-ray. The test showed that I had a duodenal ulcer. Although this condition required me to somewhat alter my eating and drinking habits, in my younger years it was easily controllable so I did not report it to the Navy, thinking that it might negatively impact my career.

I reported aboard "the Pluck" on a Sunday afternoon. The only officer aboard was Ensign Jim Ewers who was the CDO (Command Duty Officer) and the ship's Chief Engineer. The next day, I met the Captain and the other Officers: Captain (Lieutenant Commander) Robert Leopold, Executive Officer (XO) Lt. Mike Bickel, and the Operation Officer, Lt. (jg) Robert Ryerson. During the next several days I met several officers from the other four ships in our squadron. I also met my first class boatswain mate, Hendrickson, my second class storekeeper, Miller, and my second class commissary man, Countryman. Except for Miller (see Letter #2, Navy Years), these enlisted department heads were to be the back bone of my success as a Division Officer.

I hit it off with all the officers and crew. So much so that since the ship was scheduled to remain in Long Beach for refurbishment until May, I moved off the ship to a place called the Shack located in the Belmont Shores part of Long Beach. The Shack was a party place where five of us lived. Since it was located on the beach side of Ocean Avenue (literally on the sand), everyone seemed to be attracted to it. Suffice it to say, we had a great few months before going overseas.

A few highlights. On one occasion, I ended up on the Long Beach based hospital ship, "*USS Repose*", having sustained a severe gash on my nose after receiving a sucker punch from some off duty lifeguard (your typical tall, muscular, blond-haired, tanned, California beach bum) in the Anchorage Tavern, in the Marina

District of Long Beach. The guy was standing next to our table where I was with one of my shipmates and two gals from our Belmont Shore neighborhood. He was loud and boisterous and using every profanity in the book. After tolerating it for a while, I stood up and asked him if he would move to another area of the tavern. He immediately planted his fist right in my kisser knocking me into the fireplace. I got up and came after him with a vengeance, but too late. The police officer on duty and the manager came over and immediately stopped the fight. After witnesses validated that I was not at fault, the perpetrator was kicked out. Unfortunately, my gash was bleeding profusely so on to the hospital for treatment. Since Naval Officers are always gentlemen, my file showed treatment for running into a door.

On another occasion, I was driving down Ocean Avenue exceeding the speed limit late at night with four other shipmates in my car (a 1965 Chevy Super Sport I purchased while stationed in South Carolina). A squad car with two Long Beach police officers pulled us over, and the lead officer asked for my drivers' license and Navy ID (I had South Carolina license plates). While he was talking to me, the other officer asked the others if there was open beer in the car. They replied "no". Unfortunately, when asked to exit the car, one of the guys hit an open quart of beer with his foot and knocked it into the street. The lead officer than informed me that he was going to let me off with a small speeding ticket, but since my friends lied, he was going to write up speeding and open alcohol in the car. Because of the gravity of the offense, I had to go to court and the matter was reported to my commanding officer. Although the court imposed a substantial financial penalty, the Navy didn't put anything in my file, and the occupants of my car split the cost of the fine with me.

One of my duties aboard "The Pluck" was gunnery officer. As part of this responsibility, I was to lead a crew of four to pick up ammunition from the Seal Beach Ammunition Depot, about 15 nautical miles south of Long Beach. We used a Navy LCVP (a landing craft that was specifically made for marine beach assaults). We arrived at the ammo depot much earlier than anticipated, completed loading our ammo and were back in Long Beach waters before 1200. We weren't scheduled to arrive back at the ship until 1500 hours (3pm). We decided to make our own landing on the beach in front of the Shack, for a quick lunch stop. We hit the beach, lowered the LCVP's front gate, left one sailor on watch and the rest of us went up to the Shack to have some snacks and a few beers. We returned about a half hour later, got underway and arrived at the ship an hour early to unload the ammo.

It is unbelievable that no one questioned the presence of a Navy landing craft on a public beach visible to anyone walking the beach or on Ocean Boulevard adjacent to the beach. In retrospect, landing there was truly a dumb move and, as the officer in charge, I could have been in serious trouble. Nonetheless, the incident went unnoticed and no one ever found out. Thankfully, although I experienced a few unnerving issues while living off the ship, the remainder of my "on duty" naval career was by the book and it bode very well for me.

In May 1966, after six fun-filled months in Long Beach, we began our deployment to Vietnam. Our Squadron consisted of five MSO's so we set sail together, saying goodbye to my folks, Nana Helen and Papa Gus, and Mike and Pam Hosterman, who were in the Long Beach area visiting Pam's folks.

Our mission was not to sweep mines, but to participate in a secret mission at the time called "Market Time". Market Time's purpose was to set up a naval blockade in the South China Sea in South Vietnam to prevent contraband (weapons, ammunition and equipment) from being smuggled inland by the Viet Cong. A minesweeper's maximum speed was about 12 knots. However, anything above 10 knots marked mechanical trouble. MSOs were all the Navy had to use until the newly designed "Swift Boats" were completed and sent over to replace us. McHale's Navy had nothing on us!

Ensign Ruffo and Captain Leopold before Vietnam departure
Ensign Branson and me with crew departing for Vietnam

The voyage to the Western Pacific was long and grueling. As the name expresses, minesweepers (MSOs) were purpose-built ships. They were 186 feet long, made of wood, and had almost all mechanical equipment made of non-ferrous metal. Since they were not constructed for large ocean crossings, they had limited fuel capacity. So, in order to make it to our first stop, Pearl Harbor in the Hawaiian Islands, we had to put a fuel bubble on our fantail. In addition, because of the non-ferrous metal, the engines (known as Packard Diesels) were a mechanical nightmare. Consequently, there were times one or more of us were under the tow of another MSO in our transit across the Pacific.

Because they were made of wood, in a rough sea they bobbled like a cork. I can remember standing watch on the bridge with green water (a full wave rather than just spray) coming over the top of the ship. Watches were four hours long and after each watch we were assigned four hours duty in the crypto shack breaking code. After that we had eight hours to perform any department head duties and catch whatever sleep we could prior to going on watch and starting the process all over.

Many days it was literally impossible to stand without holding on to something and when the sea was extremely rough only about five or six of the crew of 60 could function at all due to sea sickness.

While standing watch on the bridge we had a bucket tied to a line attached to an overhead stanchion for vomit. The bucket maintained a relatively horizontal plane so, as long as you could hit the bucket, most of the vomit stayed in it. Sometimes the inclinometer on the bridge would show us rolling 45 degrees. Coupled with a violent pitch, the ride was very uncomfortable and downright scary. These conditions did not do much for my stomach health and it would ultimately result in my hospitalization (see detail in Letter #2, Navy Years).

The ship's wardroom where all us officer's took meals was close to the end of the mess line. Traditionally, all the officers except the officer on watch assembled in the wardroom prior to the Captain and all stood when he entered. The wardroom table was oblong and, since I had the collateral duty of supply officer, I was responsible for the commissary (the galley and provisions) and thus, was required to sit at the foot of the table facing the Captain who was obviously seated at the head. The Captain would always come down the ladder (steps) outside the wardroom and look at the mess line to see what was being served before entering the wardroom.

One day, after having been at sea for several weeks, the Captain did his usual thing, coming down the ladder from his stateroom, he noticed a five gallon container of chocolate ice cream (which he loved) at the end of the mess line being served to the crew. Upon entering the stateroom, we all came to attention and commenced our meal when the Captain was seated. The Captain made a remark that he was pleased that we were having chocolate ice cream for dessert. I gave the matter no thought, but when dessert came, the steward served him strawberry ice cream. He immediately objected saying he wanted chocolate. Our steward left and returned to tell the Captain we were out of chocolate. He became very upset, threw his napkin at me, told me never to serve a flavor of ice cream unless there was enough for everyone and left the wardroom. We were all shocked including the XO (executive officer), but had no choice except to let it pass. Captain Leopold was a tyrant and we all knew it (we called him "The Munster", because he resembled the lead character in a popular TV series, "The Munster's"). The incident reminded me of a similar story in the classic, "Mutiny on The Bounty", involving Captain Quig.

In addition to Pearl Harbor (where we could dispose of our fuel bubble), our sail plan required us to refuel at Johnson's Island, Kwajalein Atoll and enter the yards in Guam for about month of repairs. In Guam, I got involved in an incident while on shore. The military hospital held a dance during a weekend afternoon so several officers attended, including my commanding officer, the squadron commander, and all other officers of our squadron except each ship's Command Duty Officer. Of course there were other Naval Officers present, including those (males) stationed at the hospital, at the Navy base and a squadron of air dales (Navy Pilots). All-in-all there were probably 75-100 officers (all males) attending with about 30-40 Navy nurses in attendance.

After having a few drinks, I asked one of the nurses to dance. After about two or three dances, an air dale cut in on me, which I accepted. I let him dance with the gal a couple of times and then tapped him on the shoulder to cut in on him. He refused and pulled rank on me (he was a full Lieutenant and I was an Ensign). I did not take kindly to this and shoved him preparing for a full fight. The music stopped and the ruckus raised the attention of Captain Leopold, who promptly came over and ordered me back to the ship. I tried to explain the situation but to no avail so back to the ship I went. I was ultimately grounded for the remainder of our stay in port, but since it was only about three more days, it wasn't much of a punishment.

Finally, we set sail to Subic Bay, Philippine Islands for a week of refurbishment before departing to South Vietnam. Upon arrival in Subic, I became ill with my stomach condition aggravated and reported to our ship's corpsman. He sent me to the Naval Hospital for evaluation. Because of my condition, I was admitted and spent the next week in the hospital missing my ship's sailing (see page 49, for detail).

The Captain expected my return to the ship, but, much to my happiness, the hospital medical staff made the decision to med-vac (medical evacuation) me to Oakland Naval Hospital for further evaluation. While waiting for orders they transferred me to the BOQ (Bachelor Officer's Quarters) as an out-patient. Here, the Navy seemed to forget all about me. As enumerated under the US Navy chapter in Letter #2, I was transferred to Oakland and after medical evaluation was given temporary duty in San Francisco working for the Navy Seabees. Their main mission was construction. Although it was interesting work, as a line officer, I was anxiously awaiting orders to return to the fleet. In October 1966, I was assigned the "*USS Bennington*", an anti-submarine warfare carrier based out of Long Beach.

My assignment, USS Bennington, 1966-1968

I didn't know it at the time, but my Navy personnel file had been coded "red" which meant that I had political connections, presumably due to my father contacting our local politicians to have me transferred out of the Philippines to Oakland for the medical evaluation. I don't know whether this played a part in my career aboard the *Bennington* or it was my seniority and minesweeper ship handling experience, but I quickly qualified as an Officer of the Deck and, eventually became both sea detail and general quarters OOD (Officer of the Deck).

This was a real honor. I was viewed as the best ship handler among all the JOs (Junior Officers) and some senior officers who were air dales (pilots who were assigned as part of ship's company) trying to qualify as OODs. I relished this but didn't let it go to my head. In fact, once again I developed great camaraderie with my peers, my crew, and my superiors. I was assigned responsibility for Second Division. Our Division had responsibility for keeping the mid ship section of the ship shipshape, manning the high line station, maintaining the quarterdeck area, and manning the forecastle to drop and weigh anchor when necessary.

```
                    U.S.S. BENNINGTON  CVS-20        IN REPLY
                          FLEET POST OFFICE          REFER TO
                      SAN FRANCISCO, CALIFORNIA      CVS20/1310
                                                     02:JJS:djm
                                                     Ser 2894
                                                     5 OCT 1967

From:  Commanding Officer, USS BENNINGTON (CVS-20)
To:    Lieutenant (junior grade) Frank A. RUFFO JR, USNR, 691921/1105

Subj:  Officer of the Deck; qualification as

Ref:   (a) Chapter 10, Sec. 2, U. S. Navy Regulations, 1948
       (b) Art. 1003, U. S. Navy Regulations, 1948

1. As outlined in reference (a), you have demonstrated the necessary
abilities and possess the experience to perform the duties of Officer
of the Deck Underway in CVS type ships for task force steaming.

2. In accordance with reference (b), you are hereby designated as
Officer of the Deck Underway in CVS type ships.

                                        R. GRIFFY

Copy to:
BUPERS
Service Record
Ship's Secretary
Underway Senior Watch Officer
Navigator
```

My appointment as Officer of the Deck, underway, on an aircraft carrier

About a month after I reported aboard, we departed Long Beach for a seven month deployment to the Western Pacific (Westpac) to relieve another carrier in the Gulf of Tonkin off the coast of North Vietnam. A fellow officer, LT(jg) Jack Cannon, was the sea detail and GQ (General Quarters) OOD. I trained under Jack for the first part of our deployment as Junior Watch Officer. I became qualified after about a month at sea and was then assigned my own watches for the rest of the cruise (when Jack was released from active duty, I moved into his spot as the most qualified OOD on the ship).

Deploying to Westpac was a major part of our mission. Having been there on a minesweeper the year before, this was a totally different living environment. We had a relatively comfortable stateroom where four officers resided (me, Bryan Schumake, Jim Weinandy, and Lou Raisler). When underway, we rarely saw each other, since we all had responsibilities in different divisions and stood watches separately. This meant that, at any given time, one or more of us were sleeping in the stateroom so we each had to exercise diligence when awakening or retiring.

Our stateroom had a few drawbacks. First, it was located forward of the ship immediately under the starboard catapult (device that acts like a sling shot to launch aircraft). When we were conducting air operations, the noise was deafening until the entire squadron of planes was launched. Second, the General Quarters alarm was adjacent to our stateroom so when it went off, you almost levitated out of the rack (bed) from a sound sleep. Third, the ship had no air conditioning, so in the tropics, the temperature in our room remained a constant 90 to 100 degrees. We slept in our skivvies with one or no sheet. Fourth, there was only one sink, so we had to take turns if we were awakening or retiring at the same time.

Our carrier group had six destroyers so we operated together the entire time. The OOD (me when standing watch) on the aircraft carrier was responsible for giving maneuvering orders to the entire destroyer group. This was done either through voice communication or signals. Once on station, the job became fairly routine with some notable exceptions. We made port stops at Pearl Harbor (Hawaii) and Yokosuka, Japan, before deploying to the Tonkin Gulf for our first duty on station. We were assigned three periods on station: 60 days, 45 days, and 30 days, with R and R ports assigned in between.

Before entering any R and R port, a junior officer was given the collateral duty of establishing dog and pony shows for the entire crew on how to minimize catching venereal disease. Known as the "VD" officer, I was given that duty prior to entering Yokosuka. Our crew was very anxious to go ashore (I believe the appropriate term is "horny"). We steamed into the port at Yokosuka, and as the crew disembarked the ship the quarterdeck watches gave them condoms and disinfectant soap. Although the crew raised a lot of hell in town, for me, the most memorable experience was traveling by train to Tokyo, visiting the Imperial Palace and sightseeing throughout the City. After about seven days, we departed Yokosuka for our first 60 days stationed on "Yankee Station" (The Code for Gulf of Tonkin).

During our first period, we had a memorable Christmas celebration (December 26, 1966) while on Yankee Station. Bob Hope and his entire entourage came aboard to entertain us while at sea. Included were Anita Bryant; Phyllis Diller; Vic Damone; Miss World, 1966 (Reita Faria from India); Les Brown (and his band of renown); the Korean Kittens; and the biggest hit of all, Joey Heatherton. The show was on the flight deck during a dry, cloudy and very windy day with moderately rough seas. Nonetheless, Hope's group were real sports and put on a show that I have never forgotten.

I was OOD on the night watch, 2000-2400 (8PM to12 midnight) the night before the show (Christmas). It was a relatively calm night with not much going on with no air operations and all the destroyers in formation around us. All of a sudden the ship started drifting off course, which very much alarmed me because of the destroyers stationed around us. I yelled through the order tube (communication tube that connected the forward part of the bridge to the helmsman in the pilothouse behind the bridge) to the helmsman to "mind his helm" and looked through the port holes where the bridge could observe the helmsman only to see Phyllis Diller on the helm. I scolded both Phyllis and the helmsman because their actions were potentially harmful, even though they meant it in jest. I knew I could have written up the helmsman and that I was supposed to enter the incident in the log but I chose not to do either and the incident was forgotten.

Joey Heatherton created a real stir among us. When Hope's show came aboard, we had to make living arrangements for them. Many of the junior officers (ensigns and JGs) were temporarily moved out of the nicer two man staterooms to accommodate the show staff. Frank MacTernan, a fellow officer (with whom, coincidently, I attended the University of Santa Clara), had the nicest stateroom among the junior officers. He had covered his gun metal gray cabinetry with contact paper so the room had a warm, wood grain feel to it. Anyway, Ms. Heatherton was assigned to MacTernan's room for the two nights the show was aboard and he was relegated to the Chief's quarters. The word around the ship was that after Joey left, MacTernan ordered the ship's stewards not to change his sheets so he could claim he slept in Joey Heatherton's sheets. Of course, we were all envious of him.

After 60 days at Yankee Station, we steamed to Subic Bay Naval Base in the Philippine Islands. After a few days of refurbishing the ship and some well-deserved R and R, we steamed back to Yankee station for another 45 days of duty. Then, on to a great R and R port, Hong Kong. Here, we bought watches, tailor-made clothes, and stereo equipment, which we were allowed to store aboard the ship. From there, we steamed to Sasebo, Japan, for a 14 day refurbishment. The night before entering port, we were refueled by the *"USS Taluga"*, an oiler that had just left Sasebo. I knew my old high school buddy, John Egan, was an officer aboard her so I was able to make contact with him via station to station phones while the "Taluga" refueled us. John gave me all the low down about Sasebo and we ended up having a great time there. Then back to Yankee station for our final 30 days of duty.

During this last duty, I was appointed acting First Lieutenant of the ship, normally a Lt. Commander's billet (I was a senior JG, two ranks lower). The First Lieutenant was responsible for all three deck divisions, the overall appearance of the ship, and insuring that the ship was appropriately moored or anchored in every port. This was an honor and I found myself attending department head meetings with the Captain, the XO (Executive Officer) and all other department heads who were mostly commanders.

U.S.S. BENNINGTON CVS-20
MEMORANDUM

Date 13 June 1967

From: WEAPONS OFFICER

To: LTJG RUFFO

Subj: First Lieutenant (Acting); designation as

1. Until further notice you will act as the First Lieutenant and the Executive Officer will be so advised.

2. In the performance of your duties you should use the Weapons Department Organization Manual as a functional guide; and also NWP-50 and the AIRLANT/AIRPAC CV SHIP INST. Primarily, you will be responsible for the administrative and functional duties within the Deck Group and you should use any of the officers to assist you to that end.

3. A copy of this memorandum will be given to the Ship's Bos'n, who is your principal assistant in technical matters concerning the deck divisions.

4. It would appear that the ship will not have a permanent First Lieutenant assigned before September, therefore, you can be of great assistance to the new Weapons Officer in coordinating the activities of the three deck divisions.

Respectfully,

R. B. Ulm

ABOVE ASSIGNMENT IS IN ADDITION TO YOUR DUTIES AS 2ND DIV. OFFICER.

My appointment as First Lieutenant

During our periods on Yankee station we had five events that I vividly remember:
- When launching/landing aircraft at night, we were required to have a plane guard helicopter and destroyer aft in case of a crash. One night, our plane guard helicopter crashed into the sea. We immediately launched a lifeboat to look for survivors. I was in charge of the rescue operation and after lighting the area with phosphorus (which was risky because of potentially exposing us to the enemy), the only thing we found was part of one of the copter's wheel assemblies. Although the pilots were able to get out and were rescued by the plane guard destroyer, the two-man crew did not, and we never found their bodies.

- Shortly after the first incident, while a copter was landing on a spot adjacent to the bridge, it lost its tail rotor and crashed next to the bridge with its main propeller still turning and parts were flying all over including through the bridge windows. I was the OOD and I immediately hit the deck along with the Captain and others on watch on the bridge. Fortunately, there were no injuries from either the crash or the flying debris. It was determined that both incidents were caused by a faulty tail rotor assembly and all copters were grounded until the tail rotor design was modified.

- One afternoon, I was heading to the bridge to relieve the OOD when I stopped at the flight deck level to observe a wheel chocker man being crushed by the tandem wheels of a copter. He actually stood up after the wheel ran over him (like a chicken with his head cut off), and then immediately dropped, quivered a bit and then lied still. He was obviously dead. His body was placed in a stretcher and hauled off.

- On another occasion while I was OOD, we were operating in tandem with an attack carrier, the "USS Constellation". We were aft of her several thousand yards when our radar picked up a fast moving target approaching us. Although we were always at readiness condition III (a condition short of General Quarters but on alert), the target was on us about the same time as we sounded GQ. He never squawked his IFF (Identification, friend or foe), so we assumed he was the enemy. Suddenly three or four rockets exploded close to our port side, rocking the ship. If they had hit 100 yards to starboard, they would have been a direct hit to our carrier, causing severe damage if not sinking us. We learned later that it was one of our own jets that was jettisoning his payload so he could try to crash land on the "Constellation".

- Lastly, we had sent one of our destroyers, the "USS O'Brien", close to the Vietnam coast to check out suspected enemy activity. She took a direct artillery hit on her stack from an enemy encampment killing five sailors in the destroyers' engine room and severely damaging the ship. We high lined the bodies to us so we could fly them out.

At the conclusion of our Vietnam duty, we were informed that we were going to extend our Westpac cruise for a month to attend the May Coral Sea celebration in Australia. This actually was very exciting for most of the crew, including me. We steamed back to Subic Bay for provisions. When we entered port, I saw the "Taluga" at a pier so I knew Egan was there as well. We made contact and hung out together partying on Grande Island, a military recreation area in the middle of the harbor, and raising cain in the neighboring town of Olongapo, dressed in civvies, of course (the crew was required to wear uniforms ashore; officers were always in civilian clothes).

We then sailed to Sydney, Australia for a 16 day stay there. Since it was May, it was the end of the baseball season in Sydney. We received a message that the Sidney city league champions had challenged us to a baseball game while visiting. Being Yanks with baseball as our national sport, we accepted the challenge. Baseball equipment was flown aboard and Lou Raisler and I were appointed player coaches of the team. We assembled a compliment of about 20, all who had played considerable baseball and some, college ball. We practiced in the hanger deck where we could find space until we broke a windshield on an airplane and CAG (Commander Air Group) put a stop to it. That left the flight deck where we did the best we could. We obviously got minimal fielding and batting practice.

The cruise from Subic to Sydney required us to cross the equator. There is a Navy tradition that required all us pollywogs (those that had never crossed the equator) to be initiated as Shellbacks.

This is an honored tradition, but is no fun for the initiates. We were required to go through an obstacle course set up on the flight deck. The course took about 10 minutes to complete and it entailed being swatted by shellbacks, crawling through gunnysacks full of garbage, being hosed down and then kissing the bellybutton of the Shellback designated as Neptunus Rex (King Neptune). It was usually the fattest Chief on the ship and his belly button was smothered in peanut butter. Anyway, I completed the course and received my Shellback Certificate. This also becomes part of one's Navy personnel file.

Upon arrival in Sidney, my first duty as first lieutenant was to immediately go ashore as soon as the first brow was over to be sure the ship was properly moored to the dock. Once the ship was properly moored, one of the Aussie riggers came down from his crane and introduced himself to me. He immediately asked me if I would honor him by coming to "his flat" for dinner. I thanked him profusely, but that I had to decline because our superiors had scheduled the ship's officers for functions almost every evening (This was true for the first several days). Anyway, that was my first introduction to Aussie hospitality towards Americans ("Yanks", as they referred to us).

We were also greeted by the citizenry of Sydney, including many girls. The night after we arrived, the City held a formal dinner and dance for all the ship's officers (we were required to attend and wear dress whites with gloves and swords). This turned out to be a fabulous evening. Several of us met girls who we ended up dating for most of our stay. I met a gal named Jill Mie. She was very pleasant, a real lady. I dated her the entire time we were in Sydney. Jill had a girlfriend who Bryan Schumake, one of my ship mates, dated so we spent many evenings doubling. Jill introduced me to many sights of the City, including the beaches, the zoo, several parks, and, of course, the local bars and eateries.

Jill, Bryan and me, Sydney, Australia

About the third or fourth day we were in port, four of us (Mark Mahaffey, Lou Raisler, Brian Schumake and me) hired a taxi driver (cabbie, as they were called) to take us on a general tour of the City. After the tour, the cabbie took us to his private men's club where we were introduced to several members. We spent most of the afternoon drinking Aussie beer. They wouldn't hear of us paying anything for the beer. Late that afternoon, cabbie took us back to the ship.

Having received the baseball challenge, we established a daily practice routine beginning at 0630 hours until about 1000 every day, in preparation for the game which was to take place the second to the last day we were in Sydney. You can imagine the schedule we had, partying late into the night, many nights until 0200 or 0300 and then arising at 0530 for practice.

The baseball park was built for the City League and could hold about 20,000 fans. On game day, the game was scheduled to start at 1300 (1PM). Lou and I arrived early since, in addition to our baseball equipment, the Navy had purchased about 2,000 seventh fleet baseball hats to distribute to the crowd before the game. We set up a booth on the field adjacent to third base. I was the designated distributor of the hats. We couldn't believe it when fans started entering the park in droves and when they saw me giving out hats, they swarmed onto the field to retrieve one. I quickly lost control of the situation, and ended up tossing them in the air so they could fight for those that were left and to save myself from being overcome by the mob.

Believe or not, the stadium was almost full by game time. And the fans were rooting for us. The game was seven innings and, as visitors we batted first. Our best player played for the University of Michigan so we made him the leadoff hitter. On the first pitch he hit a home run, and the crowd roared. Unfortunately, that was to be our only run of the game. We just couldn't get in good enough shape with such limited practice. I ended up coaching third base rather than playing at all because I knew I was coming down with what I thought was a cough/cold. I didn't feel strong enough to play. The final score was 9-1, Sydney.

After the game, we continued to party and I participated as best I could. The day before we left I hung out with Jill, but it was obvious I was getting sicker. On departure day, Jill and all the other crew's girlfriends were waving to us from the pier as we said goodbye to Sydney. I carried out my duties as first lieutenant and was the last person to board the ship before the last brow (gangplank) was removed.

I had the first OOD watch after sea detail so when we cleared port, I relieved Jack Cannon. I was so weak that I could barely function. Captain Graffy noticed it and asked that I be relieved. I immediately reported to sick bay only to learn that I had a fever over 103 degrees and climbing, and my chest was so congested that I couldn't breathe well. Diagnosis—Pneumonia! I was immediately placed in the ship's sick bay (hospital). My temperature kept rising so the doctor had me packed in ice to try to control it. It came close to 105 degrees before it started dropping. Anyway, I became delirious and my actual memory of the event after that is a bit foggy. I do remember the doctor staying at my bedside most of the night I was packed in ice to monitor my progress. Other than that, the next thing I remembered was being allowed to walk around the hanger deck as we entered Pearl Harbor, Hawaii, about eight days after leaving Sydney. I was still too weak to go ashore. By the time we returned to Long Beach, I was back 100%. Sydney would be an R and R port I would always remember.

Like everyone else, I was anxious to return to Long Beach. While overseas, I had saved a lot of money (for me in those days). I ordered a brand new 1967 Corvette convertible which was waiting for me in Tigard, Oregon, so I was anxious to pick it up. Secondly, I had a girlfriend in Long Beach named Sally Swayze who I was anxious to see. We had been occasionally writing each other since I departed Long Beach, although I hadn't heard from her during the last three months of the cruise. When we returned to Long Beach, I found out why; she was dating someone else. I saw her a day or so after our return and she said the gentlemen had asked her to marry him, but she really wanted to marry me. Totally shocked, I told her that I was not prepared to get married so that was the end of our relationship.

After our return to Long Beach, we frequently cruised to San Diego for exercises. One memorable incident occurred when we departed San Diego Harbor for exercises off the Coast of California. We departed from North Island Naval Base (part of Coronado Island) and, I was the sea detail OOD. As we were rounding the channel to head toward Point Loma, I gave a port rudder order about five seconds later than I should have. As a result we were coming dangerously close to a buoy and small building on a dock on the starboard (right) side of the channel used to degauss ships (measure a ship's magnetic forces called a ship's signature and set the degaussing equipment on the ship to minimize the magnetism to avoid setting off magnetic mines). I had to take extraordinary steps to avoid a collision. We had way on (moving forward). Carriers had four propellers and I ordered the rudders hard to port while ordering the starboard shafts in full reverse in hopes of keeping the bow from going right and at the same time forcing the stern to left (to port).

Captain Graffy, who had a cigar in his mouth, being a man of few words, casually walked over to the starboard side of the bridge as we passed the buoy marking the beginning of the degaussing range. I was sure I took it out. Standing over the binnacle with binoculars trained ahead, smelling the aroma of the Captain's cigar, I sensed his presence standing behind me. I was nervously waiting for the bomb to hit when the Captain quietly said, "Mr. Ruffo". I replied, "Yes Sir". "You missed the buoy by four feet. Four feet is as good as four miles!" "Yes Sir, thank you, Sir". And that was the end of the incident.

During late-summer 1967, Captain Graffy was relieved by Captain Dan Murphy. Since I was the senior watch officer, Captain Murphy and I developed a close relationship. One of the Captain's first "at sea" on "*The Bennington*" was carrier qualifications being conducted off the coast of California. I was standing the second dog watch as OOD (1800-2000 or 6PM-8PM) and a Lieutenant Commander air dale was trying to qualify in an A-4 jet. He was having one heck of a time and during my watch, either I or the LOS (landing officer) waived him off because he would come in too low or too high. Another ship mate friend, Roger Adams, relieved me and I warned him about the guy.

Shortly after hitting the rack (going to bed), the GQ alarm went off. As GQ OOD, I jumped into my trousers and boots, tied my shirt around my neck, and ran up the steps to the bridge. When I passed the flight deck, I saw nothing but flames. When I got to the bridge, there was an eerie sight, the Captain in his bathrobe, Roger and the rest of the bridge crew dead silent. The Captain asked me to stand by but not to relieve Roger. Roger informed me the A-4 pilot came in too low, broke his tail hook, and severed the jet's fuselage, setting the entire angle (runway) aflame and the jet shot off the end of the angle into the sea. The pilot didn't have a chance and was likely dead before the jet hit the water.

During the first part of October, 1967, we were ordered to Pearl Harbor to prepare to retrieve Apollo 4, an unmanned space capsule that was part of NASA's quest to put a man on the moon. We left Long Beach in a dense fog and Captain Murphy ordered me to make turns for 18 knots. I cautioned the captain about the fog, but he reissued the order. As we were increasing our speed, my JO (Junior Watch Officer) reported a large contact on the radar with steady bearing and closing range (this meant potential collision). It was only about 6000 yards away (three miles). Since it takes a carrier many minutes to come to a dead stop and we were probably up to about 12 knots on our way to 18, I immediately ordered all back emergency (with the Captain's approval). I had the JO shout out the contact's ranges and bearings every 15 seconds. The fog was beginning to clear above and through it, I could see the mast of another carrier. We called it on the VHF (radio), determined it was the "USS Princeton" returning to Long Beach and, together, communicated engine and rudder orders (the "Princeton" was also in all back emergency). We came within 400 yards when the range between us started to increase. Whew, a near miss! We recorded it in the log and proceeded on our way to Pearl.

This trip was to be one of the most exciting experiences of my career (and life, for that matter). We arrived in Pearl and underwent several hours of classroom training to understand the role of each of us in retrieving Apollo 4. I was designated as OOD for the pickup. I learned that I was to be on X course 10 minutes before Apollo's appointed splash time at exact coordinates (latitude and longitude). We were also given the coordinates where Apollo would splash. We were told that at exactly Y time we would hear three loud pops at a relative bearing of 350 (10 degrees off our port bow) and we were to start looking through our binoculars for three parachutes.

Unfortunately, the weather did not cooperate at Cape Canaveral (Kennedy), so the mission kept being delayed. We sat in Pearl Harbor for over a month. Finally, on November 7, 1967, we received orders to get underway; Apollo was going to be launched during the next day or so. We arrived on station to hold several dry runs to be sure we were well-prepared for the actual recovery.

On November 9, we received word that Apollo had launched. I've included a description of the mission, courtesy of NASA:

> *The unmanned Saturn/Apollo 4 (AS-501) mission was the first all-up test of the three stage Saturn V rocket. It carried a payload of an Apollo Command and Service Module (CSM) into Earth orbit. The mission was designed to test all aspects of the Saturn V launch vehicle and also returned pictures of Earth taken by the automatic Command Module apogee camera from about one hour before to one hour after apogee. Mission objectives included testing of structural integrity, compatibility of launch vehicle and spacecraft, heat shield and thermal seal integrity, overall reentry operations, launch loads and dynamic characteristics, stage separation, launch vehicle subsystems, the emergency detection system, and mission support facilities and operations. The mission was deemed a successful test.*
>
> *Orbital insertion was achieved by ignition of the third (S-IVB) stage, putting the spacecraft (S-IVB and CSM) into a 184 x 192 km parking orbit with a period of 88.2 minutes and an inclination of 32.6 degrees. After two orbits the S-IVB was re-ignited for a simulated translunar injection burn, putting the spacecraft into an Earth-intersecting trajectory with an apogee of 17,346 km. The S-IVB stage then separated from the CSM, and the service propulsion system (SPS) ignited for 16 seconds, raising the apogee to 18,216 km. Later the SPS was re-ignited for 271 seconds to accelerate the CSM to beyond lunar trajectory return velocities. SPS cutoff was followed by separation of the Command Module (CM) from the Service Module and orientation of the CM for reentry. Atmospheric entry at 122 km occurred at a flight path angle of 7.077 degrees with a velocity of 11,140 meters/second. The CM landed near Hawaii at 20:37 UT 9 November 1967 about 16 km from the target landing point.*

Apollo 4 (Photo courtesy of NASA Images)

The Apollo Command Module splashed on November 9, at 2037 UT (Universal Time, we then referred to it as GMT or Greenwich Mean Time). This was 1037 (AM), Hawaiian time. Although the module was sighted 11,000 yards off our port bow as predicted, it was slightly more than 10 degrees to port, which required us to make a small course correction. Anyway, we came to a dead stop with the capsule about 200 yards amidships to our port. Navy divers jumped from a helicopter to immediately surround the capsule with flotation material. Small boats eased it to a spot where the ship's crane could retrieve it and we lifted it onto the flight deck. Mission completed! We steamed back to Pearl Harbor for a couple of days before returning to Long Beach.

Shortly after our return to Long Beach, there was a Naval Base Officer's Club Ball. Although many of my shipmates were planning to attend, I had no one to date. Gordy Brown, one of my ship mates had a girlfriend (and future wife) who set me up with a blind date. The gal's name was Joanne Reynolds. After the Ball, we started seeing each other regularly. In March 1968, I asked her to marry me and we set a wedding date of August 10, 1968, in Long Beach (see Letter #1 on religion for more detail).

I was due to be released from active duty in May 1968. In March, Captain Murphy summoned me to his stateroom and presented me with the opportunity to augment (become part of the regular Navy), a promotion to full Lieutenant, and orders to become Navigator on the "USS Truxton" (DLGN 35), a nuclear-powered guided missile destroyer frigate. This was a real honor and one heck of an opportunity if I wanted to make a career of the Navy. I was so taken, I asked the Captain if I could have a day or two to consider it, to which he agreed.

I gave the matter considerable thought; I knew that my father wanted me to take over the beer distributing business in Tacoma; and I was going to get married. It turned out to be an agonizing decision, but I decided to continue with my release from active duty and move back to Tacoma, primarily because of my impending marriage, the Truxton's schedule which was to deploy to Vietnam waters in June, and my perceived opportunity in the beer business.

I returned to Captain Murphy's stateroom and informed him of my decision and my reasons. He completely understood, and made a comment that I have never forgotten: "As you go through your civilian career, you will never have the amount of responsibility for life and property as you have had in your naval career!" And, although, I've had some significant responsibilities in my civilian career, Captain Murphy was right, and that was when I was in my mid-20s.

"*The Bennington*" was scheduled to leave for Vietnam on May 1 so I was released from active duty on April 30, 1968. As she left her home port at Pier Echo in Long Beach, I was standing on the pier watching her depart. It was truly a very sad and emotional experience for me as I watched "Big Ben", the ship that had been my life for the last year and a half, sail west into the sunset. And that was the end of my active naval career (Parenthetically, Captain Murphy ultimately became a four star admiral; sometimes I wonder what effect his great success and his high opinion of me may have done for me if I had chosen a naval career).

CIVILIAN LIFE TO RETIREMENT

Like every life, much occurred during the almost 40 year period in which I worked, loved, and lived the moments of my life. My purpose here is not to give a complete chronology of those years but to place emphasis on those people and events that impacted my life, both positively and negatively and how they influenced what I am today. Since the political and theological/religious aspects of my life are written separately, there will be no mention of those matters here. Here we go!

1968-1976

The summer of '68 was eventful. Joanne and I had decided to settle in the Tacoma area so I could start my career in the beer business with Dad. We decided to spend a large part of the summer living with the folks at the beach place while we found a place to live after we were married. I sold the Corvette to a navy acquaintance so we could purchase a larger car for both of us (it had 8,000 miles on it). I then flew home. Joanne joined me a couple of weeks later. We anticipated spending a couple of months at the beach before returning to Long Beach for the August wedding. We purchased a new Oldsmobile Cutlass which we intended to drive to Long Beach the end of July to prepare for our August 10 wedding.

Unfortunately, events didn't go as planned. Joanne couldn't stand living in close quarters with Mom so she decided to fly back to Long Beach after only a couple of weeks. We did find an apartment on the Gig Harbor side of the Narrows Bridge that had a beautiful view of the narrows and Mt. Rainier. After securing the apartment, Joanne returned to Long Beach and I spent the rest of the summer hanging out until the first part of August when I drove back to Long Beach.

Preparations for the wedding and reception were handled by Joanne and her mother, Annabelle. The wedding went off without a hitch except it was very hot in the church and I was pretty much a basket case the entire day. My brother, Dan, was my best man, and Joe Gonyea, one of my best friends, was in the wedding party. Dad and Mom were present along with a few of my relatives and friends from the Tacoma area. There was a reception, which I barely remember. We left the next day for our honeymoon, which was the trip up the coast back to Gig Harbor. Upon arrival we had a wedding reception at the Officer's Club at McChord Air Force base, near Tacoma. Then we both commenced work, me, with my father's company, General Beer Distributing Company, and Joanne, with the Tacoma School District at Horace Mann Elementary School.

I started working the week following the Labor Day holiday. My first day was a total surprise. Dad and his partner, Jack Walters, started arguing on the truck loading platform. The argument was over whether I should work for the Company. This was in front of all the drivers so I found it highly humiliating. It became obvious that Dad hadn't resolved this with Jack. Anyway, I lasted five weeks there with Jack unwilling to even acknowledge that I was there. In other words, he loathed my presence.

Five weeks was enough. I quit! Dad said that he would buy Jack out, but I had no clue when that would happen. Dad knew a recruiter at Weyerhaeuser Company, Bill West. He set up an interview with Bill and, Bill presented me with two opportunities—one in the Purchasing Department in Eugene, Oregon and another in the Personnel Department in Everett, Washington. I didn't even consider it a career decision since Dad believed he would work out something with the beer business and I would ultimately take it over. Since Joanne was already established in the Tacoma School District and it was closer to home, I took the personnel job in Everett. The starting salary was $700/month, starting date November, 1968.

We decided to move half way in between both commutes so from Gig Harbor we moved to an apartment close to SeaTac Airport. I commuted to Everett and Joanne commuted to Tacoma for the remainder of the 1968-69 school year.

Working for Weyerhaeuser in Everett was a good experience. I developed a close camaraderie with the personnel staff and, although I started as an interviewer for hiring hourly workers for the wood products plants, I developed a strong interest in labor relations, primarily because of the challenge of maintaining labor peace in an adversarial environment. I thought general personnel management to be rather mundane and learned that I could interact regularly with line management by learning this expertise. I was based in Everett for six years with ever-increasing responsibilities. I became Region Labor Relations Manager for Weyerhaeuser's Northern Washington Region, which encompassed all the pulp mills, sawmills woods and forest operations for Everett, White River, and Snoqualmie. This required considerable day travel by auto. I thoroughly enjoyed being out of my Everett office attending union meetings in these locations, many being in the evenings.

One person that I helped hire into Weyerhaeuser was Ed Rogel. Ed joined us in 1969, and we immediately hit it off. Our wives became friends (both ex-wives today). We spent a lot of time socializing together (several years later, Ed was instrumental in helping me through my divorce which occurred about a year following his; he also enjoyed a very successful career at Weyerhaeuser Company, retiring as Senior Vice President, Human Resources). Ed is a close friend to this day.

During the summer of 1969, Joanne had accepted a position with the Edmonds School District so we moved to an apartment just off the downtown area of Edmonds. We loved Edmonds. The town had good restaurants and shops, not to mention the beauty of the waterfront and the setting sun. I continued to commute to Weyerhaeuser Everett while Joanne now had a much closer commute. During this period of time, through Joanne's school, we met Dennis and Jean Doty and George and Joanne Wynn. We ended up being good friends and socialized together for several years.

During the fall-winter of 1970, Joanne became pregnant so we started looking for our first house. In anticipation of the arrival of our newborn, in the spring of 1971, we purchased a very nice three bedroom home in South Everett, in the Silver Lake area. We were becoming the perfect all-American family; I purchased a used station wagon; George and Joanne Wynn had introduced us to Golden Retriever's, so we purchased our dog, Ginger (eight weeks old), from a known Golden Retriever kennel in Lake Oswego, Oregon; and, we of course decorated the anticipated new arrival's room in bright yellow (I have no clue why it wasn't either blue or pink; maybe we didn't know the gender at the time).

Joanne Wynn and Jean Doty were also pregnant so it became the center of conversation for the women. Natural childbirth was in vogue so they all took Lamaze classes. Husbands were supposed to be involved so we dutifully attended the classes when required, to learn how to help our wives breath during childbirth.

During the summers of 1969, 1970 and 1971, we chartered a boat with Mike and Pam Hosterman and Gene and Jeannie Pentimonti. Although I was raised on the water and grew up around runabouts, these charters were my first introduction to pleasure boating and to the San Juan Islands. Boating was to remain part of my life to this day.

During the fall of 1971, I purchased my first boat, a 22 foot Sea Ray Weekender. It was a fast boat and during the summers of 1972 and 1973, we frequented my folks place on the Gig Harbor Peninsula (they had built a permanent residence there) and, of course made trips to the San Juan Islands and had our first exposure to the Canadian Gulf Islands.

Being Regional Labor Relations Manager for Weyerhaeuser's Northern Washington Region, I spent a large part of the spring and summer of 1971 in Portland, Oregon, as part of management's negotiating team. We ran five pulp mills in Washington and Oregon and, under a master labor agreement that expired on March 15, the Union (Association of Western Pulp and Paper Workers) struck the mills when we were unable to reach an agreement over a pension plan. Because of Joanne's impending delivery, I had flight schedules from

Portland to Seattle with me at all times. Thankfully, we settled the strike before the child was born and I returned to our Everett home.

Anyway, on August 29, 1971, our son, Brian was born at Stevens Memorial Hospital in Edmonds, Washington. Joanne ended up having a spinal block due to the pain, and I watched the birth wearing cap and surgical gown, as was required. I had always thought that a newly born baby would cry when awakened with a slap on the rear, but this was not the case with Brian. In fact, he made almost no noise as the doctor placed him on the scale which led me to believe there was a problem. The doctor assured me that he was fine.

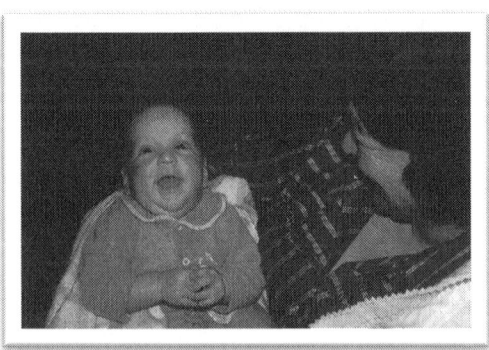

Baby Brian with me, Mom, and Papa Gus, 1971
Brian and Mom, 1971

In the fall/winter of 1973-74, I accepted a corporate position as Assistant Western Division Labor Relations Manager, based out of Weyerhaeuser's corporate office in Federal Way, Washington.

I reported to Dave Reynolds, the Western Labor Relations Manager. We purchased a nice rambler in Federal Way, Washington, and were fortunate to have a quick sale of our Everett home. At this point, I notified Dad I had no interest in entering the beer business so he should sell it to an outsider

We lived in a community called Mar Cheri. As part of the community, we had a beautiful gated, almost Olympic-size swimming pool close to our house. It was very convenient for us. We organized swimming lessons for the kids and frequently had neighborhood parties. On one Saturday afternoon party, everyone was eating, drinking beer and having a great time when we saw a body at the bottom of the pool. It was one of those incidents frozen in time. Our pool lifeguard was present and immediately jumped in to rescue the child. It was our four year old son, Brian! After considerable coughing, choking, and sobbing, the lifeguard took Brian right back into the pool and walked him around the shallow end for almost a half an hour. This was a great move; Brian became an outstanding swimmer and ultimately, worked as a life guard himself.

Corporate Weyerhaeuser was another story. Politics were rampant; it seemed like everyone was at each other's throats and I found the environment not to my liking. The physical plant was state of the art for its day; no offices, but open space to accommodate modern-looking cubicles All employees kowtowed to the fifth floor where senior management officed. Dave was an excellent negotiator but he had a mysterious personality. He was a man of few words except at the bargaining table, where he would frequently expound that he was "just an old country boy" (Dave was from Arkansas). In short, I learned a lot about bargaining technique just by watching him in action, but our different personalities (me, being an extrovert and Dave, an introvert) made it difficult for us to develop a close friendship.

In 1975, an opportunity presented itself that became one of my greatest corporate learning experiences. We had a box plant in

Honolulu, Hawaii. The employees were represented by the Longshoreman's Union. Although I would have loved to have the assignment to be able to visit the Islands again and bring Joanne to mix business with a little vacation, Dave took it himself presumably for the same reason.

In the Pacific Northwest, a big issue was developing for all of Weyerhaeuser's timberlands. The logging industry had a long-established practice of assigning two cutters to every tree to be cut, based on the early industry practice of using a large double saw with cutters manning both ends. With the advent of chain saws the practice continued and Weyerhaeuser decided it needed to be stopped. This would cut labor costs almost in half.

Since Dave was in Hawaii negotiating the box plant contract, Timberland management came to me. Together, we put together a proposal to present to the IWA (International Woodworkers of America). At age 33, I was to be the spokesperson for Weyerhaeuser in this matter. My first task was to contact the union president, a man named "Gundy" Gundvalson. Gundy was a crusty guy, of formidable physical stature who grew up in the industry. I set up our first meeting with him privately in his office in Portland.

At the meeting, I gave him our proposal. After a quick review he said it would never fly because of the large number of jobs lost. I asked him if it would receive his support if we somehow addressed the job loss issue. He said he would listen. We set up subsequent meetings with an expanded group including additional union and management representatives.

After several deliberations and caucuses, Gundy and I reached an agreement that he would sell to the membership. We would eliminate the junior cutter from any tree 36 inches in diameter or smaller; we would increase the remaining cutter's hourly wage by $1.00; we would move the junior cutter to another position in the Company in the same crew, but at the rate of the new job. The proposal was accepted!

I became a hero in the eyes of Timberland management and received thanks from senior management. Unfortunately, this didn't seem to play well with Dave Reynolds! Our questionable relationship started to deteriorate further. In the fall of 1975, in a private meeting, Dave asked me to find another position in Weyerhaeuser and suggested I interview for the Region Personnel Manager opening for the Southeastern Division based in New Bern, North Carolina. He also said there was no hurry and that I could take up to six months to find something else within the Company.

I was devastated, but quickly learned that he had covered his decision with management so my goose was cooked. I called my good friend, Mike Hosterman. He suggested that I contact Rich Hosking, a psychological business and personal consultant that he used. I made contact with Rich and signed up for one of his seminars. This turned out to be a great move; it had a major influence on my career path and on my decision-making process going forward.

The seminar was four days long conducted on Rich's 53' sailboat with no more than eight attendees. The exercises in Rich's course brought to light how I was a total mismatch for large corporate life and I needed more freedom to make decisions on my own. After the seminar I made the decision to leave Weyerhaeuser and use the remainder of my six month period to find a position outside the Company.

I met with Scott Witt, the Vice President of Personnel, and informed him that I no longer wanted to find a position within Weyerhaeuser, but I would be searching for a position like his in a much smaller company. Scott was a great guy; he completely understood and wished me luck. Two days later, he summoned me to his office. I wondered, "What now"? Scott said that he was on the Board of the Tacoma Art Museum, and that at last night's meeting, another board member, Dan Baty, who was president of the Hillhaven Corporation based in Tacoma, was looking for an employee relations director with strong labor relations skill. Scott gave Dan my name only to learn that Dan and I had known each other since high school days. Dan asked Scott to have me call him.

The next day, I called Dan; we set up an interview for a couple of days later and, after being interviewed by the Company's CFO and VP of Professional Services, he hired me on the spot. Thus, in March 1976, I began my new career in health care where I would spend the rest of my working days.

1976-1989

The Hillhaven Corporation was a nursing home company that had just recently grown from 30 facilities to 65. Dan wanted me to start as quickly as possible since a major labor contract encompassing 22 facilities in California was going to expire in June. Weyerhaeuser Company let me leave without the traditional two weeks' notice, so I left with a flowering letter of recommendation and started work at Hillhaven the following Monday as Employee Relations Director.

The corporate office was in Tacoma so the commute from our Federal Way home was a piece of cake. Jim Gaddis, who had been Employee Relations Director, had resigned to take a consulting position in California. Jim stayed on for a couple of weeks to orient me. We flew to San Francisco to meet the local management and union leaders. He also introduced me to the employee relations staff comprised of three young females - Eileen, Jeannie, and Debra.

When I left Weyerhaeuser, I had copied Weyerhaeuser's entire personnel and administrative policy manual. Since Hillhaven had almost no organized personnel policy, I spent hours revising the Weyerhaeuser policies to fit the Company. I sold senior management on implementing the policies and then introduced them to the field. I had divided the employee groups into three categories with the "unique" classifications of Category I: corporate/regional staff, facility administrators, and directors of nursing; Category II: facility department heads; Category III: facility employees. We structured policies and benefits to fit each category with the basic philosophy that Category I policies/benefits would be uniform throughout the company (for portability), and Category II and III policies/benefits could be different based on competitive issues in each locale (however, it made sense to standardize as much as possible for administrative ease).

Everything seemed to be going smoothly. We settled on a three year labor agreement in California and fully implemented our company policies. One day, Dan summoned me to his office and told me that he just had a meeting with three very distraught ladies—my staff! They had told Dan that they were having difficulty communicating with me and that I was "stand offish". I immediately met with all three of the ladies both collectively and individually to ask them what we could do to improve communication. The meetings were very fruitful and, as a result, we agreed to have weekly meetings to air any issues. To my knowledge, we never had any other major communications problems after that (with the current staff).

During 1976, I was diagnosed with mild hypertension. To this point, I hadn't paid much attention to my physical health and consequently, I was overweight, and in generally poor condition for a 34 year old. This diagnosis shook me up. I immediately started on an active exercise program that included daily running and being conscientious of what I ate. It paid off. I lost 30 pounds and, although I would be taking blood pressure medication the rest of my life, it was controllable, and I felt great.

Joanne and I were trying to have a second child with no success. So we decided to adopt a baby girl. We contacted Catholic Children Services and made application. It took a little time to receive approval, but the Services contacted us in late January, 1977, to let us know that a baby girl had been born on January 19 and she seemed a perfect fit for our family. We had already picked the name, "Christina Marie", and learned that the foster parents (who under Service policy, were required to keep her for two months), had given her the temporary name of Christine Elizabeth. We initiated action to have her birth certificate changed to Christina Marie and received this wonderful gift about the third week in March, 1977.

Infant Christina, 1977   *Tina with Brian, 1977*

Tina was totally different from Brian. Whereas Brian slept most of the day and kept us awake many nights, Tina was a holy terror during the day but was usually totally exhausted at night. Tina was extremely outgoing and Brian was on the more reserved side. (Interestingly, as they became adults, they seemed to reverse roles). On one occasion, we had dinner guests at our Federal Way home and two year old Tina, who we thought was comfortably tucked in bed, suddenly appeared at the top of our living room steps buck naked, raised her arms in the air, and shouted "Ta Da!" Everyone howled. Those were fun days.

Business life was going well. Although one of my key staff, Eileen (Butkus) resigned to follow her husband's military transfer to the East Coast, it gave me the opportunity to hire a replacement with a little more experience. I filled it with a lady named Vicki Childs, who turned out to be a mixed bag. Her on the job performance was exemplary, but Vicki was an emotional mess. She succeeded in capturing the attention of senior management because of her excellent skills, but she was a gossip and politicized virtually everything. Right after she was hired she informed me that her husband was black, which she apparently thought was a big deal to let us know. Ultimately, it became a battle between her and I as to who would stay with the Company, but it would be several years before this would happen.

In keeping with Dan's style, the company was growing rapidly. After about six months, I was appointed Vice President-Administration along with two other appointments: Nick Gerde, CFO; and Jan Tietjen, COO. As part of this promotion, Dan approved the building of three offices to accommodate our new status. One day, while I was on a business trip, Vicki called to inform me that Dan had ordered the offices torn down and made smaller. Apparently, he had the offices measured and determined that they were slightly bigger than his (or Neal Elliott's, the CFO and John Hackley's, the VP of Professional Services). With my tail between my legs, I flew home, apologized, and completed construction of smaller offices with no political fallout other than embarrassment.

The years after 1976 saw extremely rapid growth. Through several acquisitions, by 1986, the company grew from about 65 facilities when I joined it, to 430 facilities in 33 states. We were a billion dollar company with over 30,000 employees. Life was good. In addition to human resources, during that period, I had assumed responsibility for risk management, purchasing, dietary, public relations, professional services and corporate office administration.

This added responsibility and future growth did not come without its challenges. The first acquisition that I was involved with was First Healthcare East. As with almost all acquisitions, there was conflict between egos of both managements with the acquired Company believing its people and systems were superior to the acquirer's. In my case, this involved a lot of negotiation with the First Healthcare President, a gentleman named Marvin Wilensky, who would remain with the Company as Vice President, Operations of our new Northeastern Division and, ultimately, with the departure of Jan Tietjen to a competitor, of our entire Company's operations.

Over a period from August 1976 to December 1977, Marvin and I gradually built a trusting relationship and, based on many of his suggestions and cooperation, we made several changes, including changing the name of the Boston (Lexington) First Healthcare office to Hillhaven; adopting Hillhaven's Human Resources policies and benefits; replacing my Public Relations Director with Marvin's, reporting to me; replacing our labor council with Marvin's and, when Marvin was appointed Senior Vice President of Operations, placing purchasing/dietary under his control. At the same time as Marvin's promotion, John Hackley retired, I was made Senior Vice President and I promoted Vicki to Vice President, Human Resources. Through all this, I was chief labor relations strategist and sometimes negotiator, receiving legal advice from Jackson Lewis, a law firm that I was to have a close, personal relationship with for the remainder of my career.

My Promotion to Senior Vice President

Suffice it to say, there was a lot of stress and challenges as we went through this growth, but the greatest challenge facing the company and senior management occurred on April 2, 1978 (Joanne's birthday). We had concluded a major acquisition of the 60 facility Merit Corporation on April 1. In doing so, we retired the Company's existing stock and floated a new issue as a result of the merger. The next day, East Coast-based Manor Care made a hostile tender offer on our stock. I had just started a vacation on the Oregon Coast with my family when I got a call from Vicki as to what had happened. Although I completed my vacation, my mind was elsewhere. I returned to a very unsettled company with everyone wondering what was in store for us.

During the next 21 months, I was to experience many offensive and defensive maneuvers from each side with Hillhaven trying to remain independent and Manor Care trying to control the company. We floated voting preferred shares and issued them to Louisville-based Hospital Affiliates; Manor Care filed a law suit; we countered by raising the bid on our own stock; Manor Care bid the stock up further, and on and on for several months. At one time we talked about splitting the company up with us retaining the Northeast and California with Manor Care taking the rest.

During this period, we were uncertain what direction our personal careers might go. In spite of the uncertainty, Joanne and I decided to purchase a larger home. We found a beautiful Tudor style home that had just begun construction so we were able to influence the design and selection of materials for completing the house. The home was completed in the spring of 1979. We were able to make a quick sale of our Federal Way home and we moved into our new home in Edgewood, a suburb of Puyallup, Washington. The home was spacious, being over 5,000 square feet. We thoroughly enjoyed it with its large bedrooms for the kids, a monstrous master bedroom, an office for me, a large recreation room, and a large fenced yard for the kids and our dog, Ginger.

Our Edgewood home, 1979

Joanne, Brian, Tina, and me, 1978

Regarding the company, splitting it up became unnecessary. Fortunately for us, National Medical Enterprises, a large mainly acute hospital company based out of Santa Monica, California (now Tenet Healthcare), worked out a deal with all the parties, whereby they would become Hillhaven's "White Knight". NME, as they were known then, would purchase all the outstanding shares of Hillhaven; we would become a wholly owned subsidiary; and NME would retain Hillhaven management and the Tacoma base as is. On January 1, 1980, Hillhaven became NME's Long Term Care Group, soon to take management responsibility for the 15 nursing homes they had operated.

As a result of Hillhaven's purchase by NME, Dan became CEO of the Long Term Care Group and Neal Elliott was promoted to President. Marvin Wilensky was promoted to COO of the nursing home division. We hired two new operating Vice Presidents, one to operate our Western Division (Andy Turner), and the other as the new CFO (Klem Belt). The NME relationship was great; Hillhaven was doing very well financially so NME Senior Management let us run the show. I developed a great working relationship with NME's Senior VP of Human Resources and his staff. This bode well for members of Hillhaven's senior management since I was able to negotiate salaries and bonuses for our whole team.

In November, 1980, I was searching for an administrative assistant. After reviewing several resumes, I was unable to find anyone who I felt to be a good fit. I routinely screened out anyone who worked for a government entity since my vision of them was they were generally lifers who expected a large salary and benefit package with minimal work effort. In frustration, I asked Andy Harris, a member of our human resources staff, to review all the resumes and narrow it down to two or three. I then left for a scheduled vacation prior to the long Thanksgiving holiday weekend.

A day or so later, Andy called me and said he had three people he had phone interviewed, and wanted me to interview one of them. I asked him about her credentials and he stated she was a fast typist, could take excellent shorthand, and had experience in human resources management. He also said she worked for the Soldiers Home in Orting, which was a government agency. Because of this, I was skeptical, but I agreed to an interview. Because of my sense of urgency to find an assistant, I came in off of vacation for the interview. After the interview, I came away impressed. We extended an offer to her and she began working as my Administrative Assistant the first week in January, 1981. Her name was Sandy Christensen. Because of her talents, Sandy only worked for me for a short period before being offered a job in employee relations, first on the corporate staff, reporting to Vicki Childs; then as Regional Employee Director for California (of course, then, I had no idea that Sandy would someday become my wife!).

In 1982, we had decided to move the corporate office from our Center Street location to downtown Tacoma. We moved into an older building that had been completely gutted and made into beautiful, plush office space. I had a spacious corner office at the end of the building. This was professional environs at its best!

The next eight years was to be a period of growth for me professionally. This was not the case personally. Although I had become an avid runner and stayed in outstanding physical shape, my emotional commitment to Joanne started to wane. My position with Hillhaven required frequent travel. Although I tried to be involved in family activities by becoming cub master of Brian's cub pack and purchasing a boat, a 1971, 34' Tollycraft sedan, I found myself gone a lot and unable to devote the time that I should have with the family. Joanne became increasingly critical of my frequent absences. Our relationship deteriorated further. Joanne had taken the role of mother to me as well as the kids. It became increasingly difficult for me to come home. We began to argue more frequently. By 1982, our home had become a prison for me rather than a sanctuary. During this year we also had to put Ginger down, which was very difficult for our family. This was not a pleasant time (see Letter #1 regarding some of the issues that caused additional havoc on our marriage).

In 1982, Joanne and I took a vacation trip to Maui. We had previously traveled to Maui in 1978 with our friends, Duncan and Julie McMillan, when we were introduced to the Hale Hue Kai condos in Kihei. On the first or second day of our trip, while playing tennis, I tore my medial meniscus in my right knee. As a result, I had to be air lifted to Honolulu. We had made arrangements through Joanne's friends who lived on Oahu, Chris and Sharon Smith, to meet Kent Davenport, an orthopedic surgeon, who would perform orthoscopic surgery on the knee. I checked into Queens Memorial Hospital where the surgery was performed. After my release, I recuperated at Chris and Sharon's home for about 10 days. Joanne apparently felt my injury robbed her and told me that, "I had ruined her vacation." I never forgot that comment.

In February, 1982, my grandfather, Papa Gus, died after a lengthy illness. His funeral was at St Rita's Italian parish in Tacoma. Prior to his death, there was a rift growing between my grandmother's (Nana Helen) family and Mom and her sisters. Nana Helen was Papa's third wife, the other two had died; the first one in Italy (Mom's mother); the second, here, as a result of an acute infection. Nana and Papa

Nana Helen and Papa Gus, 1974

Nana Helen and Papa Gus, 1979

were married about the same time as Dad and Mom, so Nana Helen was the only grandmother I knew.

Papa had decided to be buried next to his second wife, Mary. Although he left the house to Nana, he gave his half of the cash in the estate to his three daughters (Aunt Barbara, Mom, and Aunt Rose), a mere $21,000 (a substantial sum at the time). These provisions in his will split the family. Before the funeral mass began, I went into the sacristy to ask the celebrant, Fr. John McDonald, who I had known at Bellarmine, if I could say a few words after the Mass. He said he would call on me.

At the end of the Mass, Fr. McDonald nodded towards me; I went to the pulpit and gave an impassioned sermon on how Papa would not have wanted this dispute, but was only trying to do what was in his heart. We have been one family all our lives and this should continue.

In subsequent days, I learned that the Orlando clan (Nana's side of the family) believed that this was a ploy planned well in advance. They refused to talk to us any further and ask that I not visit Nana ever again. Since she was the only grandmother I ever knew, I did not live up to that! I visited her on at least one occasion shortly before her death. When Nana died, the Orlando clan made it clear they did not want us to attend her funeral. I debated whether to defy their wishes, but, at the urging of Mom and Dad, I chose not to rock the boat and stayed clear. I still feel anger and hurt today when I think about this.

"Forgive and forget did not come easy to me!"

Joanne and I continued to have marital problems into 1983. I felt more and more like a prisoner as time went on and, therefore stayed on the road as much as possible. As a result of some previous indiscretions on my part (see Letter #1) as well as continued loss of feeling for her, we separated on November 11, 1983.

I moved into an apartment across the valley on Puyallup's South Hill. I took my clothes and one television with me and that was about it. I had to rent furniture and bought some press board shelving for the TV and a few books. The place was a real hole. It reeked of chemical cleaner to cover up several years of cigarette smoke so when the kids stayed with me (in rented bunk beds), Joanne always complained their clothes smelled of smoke. We entered into counseling, but my heart wouldn't allow me to go back to what I considered a failed relationship so about mid-1984, I filed for divorce (see more detail in Letter #1).

After I filed I looked for a more comfortable place where I knew I was likely to live for quite some time. Ed Rogel from Weyerhaeuser days had been divorced and lived in a very nice apartment not too far from the sleaze hole I lived in so I rented a place in the same complex as Ed. These were nice apartments. Since I thought that I was starting a new life I began buying furniture, kitchen equipment and whatever to make the apartment a true home. Here, I was at peace, but outside circumstances continued to assail my peace.

In December, 1983, I took Sandy to Seattle on our first date. I was extremely nervous since it had been only one and a half months since Joanne and I separated. We went to dinner at Elliott's Restaurant on Seattle's waterfront. Of course, I thought everyone in the restaurant knew me and saw me with a strange woman! As I noted in Letter #1, Joanne and I went through counseling, but I never had my heart in fixing our marriage. I continued to date Sandy somewhat clandestinely; only close friends and business associates were aware of our growing relationship (Mike Hosterman, and Ed Rogel, both divorced and dating other women; Duncan and Julie McMillan, who kept a boat at the same marina as me and saw me coming home from a weekend trip with Sandy); Dan Baty, Neal Elliott, and, of course, Sandy's boss, Vicki Childs).

Even though I was still attending counseling sessions, Sandy and I began seeing each other quite often. In July, 1984, I invited her on a vacation boat cruise on my 34' Tollycraft to the San Juan and Gulf Islands. Sandy had never cruised on a boat. I told her, "This would be the trip of her life!" Little did I know how clairvoyant I was.

Sandy and I aboard "Sunrise"

"Sunrise" 1984

On July 25, we left Totem Marina in Tacoma for what was to be a two week trip to the Islands. I refueled with 225 gallons of gasoline prior to departing. It was a beautiful, sunny July day and we were together on the flying bridge of the *"Sunrise"* (the boat's name) cruising just passed the ferry landing at Clinton on Whidbey Island when catastrophe hit.

The starboard engine suddenly quit and smoke started billowing from the cock pit. I immediately scurried down the bridge ladder and barely opened the engine room hatch; having filled the engine room with more oxygen, flames started shooting out of the hatch. I panicked due to the amount of gasoline aboard and was sure the boat was about to explode. I yelled to Sandy to come down from the bridge and told her we needed to jump overboard. Because of my sense of urgency and being unable to reach life jackets due to the smoke in the cabin, I jumped into the sea. Sandy teetered on the gunwale and asked if she should jump. Realizing we had no flotation device, I said, "Throw the life ring (mounted on the port side) in and then jump in."

Sandy threw the ring in and then jumped. We both had one arm through the donut hole of the life ring which kept us afloat quite well. Being reasonably close to land, I felt we could easily swim to shore or, worse case, be picked up by the Clinton Ferry. Neither proved to be the case. The current was too strong to make any headway swimming and we had drifted out of the ferry lane so no one could see us (Thank God; not seeing us, the captain would have likely run us over). Shortly after we jumped, the boat's Halon fire retardant system went off and the fire went out. Unfortunately, we had no way to return to the boat because of the strong current.

I decided our only hope was to be rescued by a passing boat, but the seas were becoming increasingly rough and there were no boats in sight. We pulled our knees up close to our bodies to preserve heat. At this point, I concluded we were likely goners and stated, "God damn it; she's going to get it all!" (Meaning Joanne would inherit my estate, for what it was worth in those days)

Finally, we saw a small cruiser coming right for us. As she approached, she suddenly changed course slightly away from us. Sandy started yelling at the top of her lungs; the three startled men aboard had heard her yell and slowly approached us. Not knowing how to get us out of the water, they finally grabbed each of us and used sheer muscle power to pull us onto the boat. After close to an hour in the water and due to being an avid runner with low body fat, I started uncontrollable shivering from hypothermia. Although Sandy was thin, she fared much better because of the higher level of body fat naturally in women, even in her great shape.

Anyway, Sandy suffered sea sickness due to the rough seas. The men wrapped me in a blanket, placed me in the boat's v-birth and gave me a shot of vodka. This was a big no-no! I immediately went into convulsions. Meanwhile, *"Sunrise"* had floated away from us so the guys saw her, took her in tow and brought us into Everett, Washington. They wanted to take us to the local hospital but I said no. By then several hours had passed and both of us were almost fully recovered. We had the men drop us off at a car rental agency. Although I had a wet wallet, I did have ID and a credit card. We rented a car and went to a local Motel 6 for the night. We had dinner at a nearby restaurant and celebrated the fact we were alive with a stiff drink or two, wine and a fine steak! The next day we drove back to Tacoma.

We were able to continue our vacation with our close friends, Duncan and Julie McMillan, who graciously offered to have us go with them on their 42' Cruise-A-Home, *"Free Spirit"*. So, for the first time, Sandy was able to experience the San Juan Islands after all (after we purchased our new vessel, *"Island Mist"*, Duncan and Julie would be cruising with us for many summers over the next several years).

My divorce proceedings were not going well. Joanne had hired an attorney named Ed Harmaan to handle the proceedings. In my ignorance I thought this would be a simple procedure. I met with Ed and, although he seemed to be willing to work with me, he made it clear the he was Joanne's attorney.

How true this became. While I was on a business trip, Mr. Harmaan instructed Joanne to empty all of our bank accounts and put the money in a personal account in her name. I returned from my business trip only to find out after trying to write a check that there was zero balance in the account. No communication from Joanne at all! This was dirty pool! I, of course, immediately hired my own divorce attorney and was forced to ask for an advance on my own salary for daily living expenses. As a senior vice president of Hillhaven, I experienced considerable embarrassment.

I do not blame Joanne for withdrawing the money, but Harmaan became one of the biggest jerks in my life at that point in time (unfortunately, he wasn't to be the last). Of course, he will claim he was merely protecting his client, and, although I've seen him in various restaurants in Gig Harbor from time to time (he doesn't appear to remember me), today, I realize he was merely doing his job and I have moved on.

The divorce then became war for me (thanks Ed). I just wanted to get on with my life. To do that, I decided to give up whatever I had then to protect my future. Without getting specific, Joanne got a lot and I started over. Thankfully, with perseverance and considerable luck, I prevailed and, after many anxious years, this strategy paid off big time.

Our divorce became final in July 1985, one year and nine months after we separated. Even though I had very little assets remaining, because of my high salary, the decree required me to pay substantial alimony, child support and for Joanne's Master's degree at Pacific Lutheran (close to $5000 per month). Nonetheless, I finally was able to get on with my life. Using almost all credit except for a loan from my folks (most of which I ultimately paid back), I bought a new car (Jeep Cherokee to replace the 280 ZX that had no room for the kids); I ordered a new boat (sold my 34 Tollycraft, given the bad experience of the previous summer and purchased a 42' Ponderosa to be delivered the following March); I purchased a waterfront home close to our old summer place where I had fond childhood memories; and, although, Sandy and I had been dating for quite some time, it became much more comfortable being with her in public.

The year 1986 brought a turning point in the nursing home industry. Because of the passage of government legislation further regulating the industry our profits started to fall. As a result, NME became much more involved in our operations. This did not sit well with Dan Baty. He and Dick Eamer, the NME CEO, apparently got into a dispute. Consequently, in March, 1986, Dan cut a deal and left the Company. Neal Elliott succeeded him as CEO of NME's Long Term Care Group.

Neal's tenure would not last six months. Neal had wanted a special retirement package from NME which Eamer refused to provide. Trying to keep his intent under the radar, Neal decided to form another company and brought Andy Turner and Klem Belt in on the deal. Secretly, the three of them began to organize their own company.

Meanwhile, I continued to have trouble with Vicki Childs. She had developed such an ego that she thought she could do no wrong. It became clear that her intent was to undermine me. In June, 1986, while together on a business trip in San Diego, Vicki became intoxicated and told me that I was in trouble with Neal and that I was likely out. Here was an employee that I had hired, promoted and supported pulling the rug out from under me. I was incensed and told her that she was to stay in San Diego to complete our business and that I was flying home the next morning to have a discussion with Neal regarding her comment. I then retired to my hotel room.

About 2AM, I was awakened with a feeble knock on my room door. I quickly put on some trousers and opened the door. There stood a completely disheveled and intoxicated Vicki asking if she could come in to have a discussion. I let her in and she proceeded to back track on her comments. She obviously knew she was in trouble. I thanked her for her "clarification" and told her I intended to proceed as planned and fly home for the discussion with Neal. I then excused her.

The next morning I called Neal to tell him I was flying home and wanted to meet with him. When I arrived at corporate, I went immediately to Neal's office and let him know what Vicki had said. Neal denied any of her comments were true. I then told him that she had to go and I intended to fire her. He agreed that she was a problem and that I had his blessing (I believe the real reason Neal was so agreeable was that he had likely already decided to hire her into his own company, which he ultimately did when he left).

Vicki's departure was a relief for me. I decided not to replace her immediately to see what opportunities might unfold. I had already split responsibility for salary administration and the Benefits Department from Vicki, since her real skill lie in the training and policy area. So I placed Deb Cieplik, who had been in my organization since I joined Hillhaven, in charge of the corporate HR staff.

In March of 1986, I took delivery of my 42' Ponderosa yacht and spent most of my spare time commissioning it. By August, it was ready for its first cruise. One of the Company matters that was left undone was the termination of Dan Platt, who was President of our recently formed retirement housing division. Platt had totally mismanaged the division. Neal knew I had planned the summer cruise on our new boat so he told me to go on with it and he would handle the Platt issue.

Our first "Island Mist" 1986-2004

With Sandy and son, Brian, aboard, we departed for the San Juan and Gulf Islands in our new boat, the *"Island Mist."* We had been underway for about 10 days. We were moored at Telegraph Harbor Marina on Thetis Island when I phoned the office from the Marina pay telephone (there were no cell phones then). Speaking to Neal, I asked "How did it go" (meaning the Platt termination)? He said, "Not well. Everyone was in shock. I am taking Andy and Klem with me as well!" I was aghast. I had been talking about Dan Platt and Neal had announced he was leaving to form his own company. I tried to act calm and asked him when the effective date was. He said, "Immediately." When I asked about the Platt termination, he said that it was taken care of.

I called Marvin Wilensky in Boston. He said Eamer had already been in touch with him. He (Eamer) also had decided to promote Bruce Busby, who Dan had originally brought into Tacoma as VP of our Ancillary Group (other companies outside the nursing home group) as President of the Long Term Care Group. NME had negotiated a two year deal with Marvin as President of Hillhaven reporting to Busby. I would be reporting to Marvin. Marvin instructed me to return to the office as quickly as possible and he would meet me in Tacoma. We departed Telegraph Harbor and set course for Anacortes, Washington, where I would temporarily leave "*Island Mist*" and rent a car to drive us to Tacoma.

As the only officer left in the Tacoma office, I held an all-staff meeting and explained what had taken place and what our new organization was going to be. I then immediately stopped Neal's, Andy Turner's and Klem Belt's salaries and benefits (illegal, but I didn't care). Klem accused me of being "underhanded and low down" but I shouted right back that they left the company in a big hole and that was what they deserved. It took them appealing to NME's General Counsel, Mark Powers, to finally receive the remainder of their salaries.

Neal formed Horizon Healthcare with Andy running operations and Klem, finance. They temporarily opened up shop down the street from us. They intended to hire away specific employees from our staff. To my surprise, they hired Vicki Childs as VP Human Resources (Andy hated Vicki while at Hillhaven), and Randi Nathanson, whom I had just fired as our Corporate Counsel, as their General Counsel (parenthetically, this was one of the toughest terminations I ever had to make. I was instrumental in bringing Randi into the Company, having hired her on a project in Milwaukee when she was an intern working for one of the East Coast law firms we used. In this case, I was only the messenger; our management believed she had allegiance to Neal and instructed me to carry out her termination; thankfully, years later, we used her extensively when she established her own Seattle-based law practice and I became a co-founder of the Emeritus Corporation).

Anyway, we reorganized the company appointing three Senior Vice Presidents of Operations (Geisinger, Mosca, and Pierce). I became Senior Vice President, Administration. The next two years were both fun and challenging; the industry was not doing well, but our senior management team got along exceptionally well. We rehired Bob Pacquer as CFO. Years before, Dan and Neal had fired Bob as CFO of Hillhaven; he had formed his own accounting practice that I used for personal tax accounting and was glad to see him back. We also hired Rich Adcock from NME's legal staff as General Counsel. This completed our management team.

In the fall of 1986, as previously mentioned, I purchased a waterfront home on Shaw's Cove on the Gig Harbor peninsula close to where I spent my youthful summer days. Sandy and I had decided to marry so we looked for several weeks before selecting the home on Horsehead Bay Drive. She was instrumental in decorating the house and made it a true home. On May 2, 1987, we were married in the home. I had Mike Hosterman, Duncan McMillan, and Ed Rogel, all close friends who were extremely supportive through my divorce, stand with me for the ceremony. (see Letter #1 on marriage particulars).

Our New home, fall 1986

Our marriage at our home, May 2, 1987

After our marriage, we celebrated our honeymoon on the Hawaiian Islands; first in Oahu and then Maui. When we arrived at the Turtle Bay Hilton on the north side of Oahu, it was very warm so we headed to the barefoot bar next to the pool for Mai Tai's. Unfortunately, I drank too many and found myself beyond drunk. The only love I made that night was to the toilet in spite of the wonderful cheese plate and wine the Hotel had provided through arrangements made by my Hillhaven colleagues and my travel agency.

"Touché!"

After our return home, we had decided that Sandy could no longer work for Hillhaven since she was now the wife of a senior officer. She made the decision to return to school to study for her four year RN degree. She matriculated at Tacoma Community College for her prerequisites and finished her degree at Pacific Lutheran University, graduating in the 1992 class.

At the last minute, son Brian had decided to attend Bellarmine Prep in Tacoma. After calling the President, Fr. Dan Weber, I was able to have him enrolled. Financially, this meant that besides my responsibilities under the divorce decree, I was now paying for a new wife's education, a son's tuition at a private high school, and a $2,000/month mortgage on our new home. Although money was tight, the timing was right for me to rebuild. My high salary was allowing me to support all this.

As soon as he turned 16, which was during August, 1987, before the beginning of his sophomore year, Brian decided to live with us. I bought him a car so he could drive himself. Big mistake. In May, 1988, towards the end of his sophomore year, he had talked me into allowing him to buy a radar detector with the argument there were a lot of traps between our house and school. His real motive was to participate in a race from Gig Harbor to Ocean Shores and back against Luke Xitco, another classmate. Unfortunately, Brian didn't make it to Ocean Shores. After being observed but not caught by the Washington State Patrol, he eventually rolled his car down an embankment on a hair pin turn outside of Hoquiam, Washington. He ended up with a totaled brand new Ford Tempo, received a minor knee injury and after a night in the hospital, was driven home by his buddies. Was he lucky! The vehicle's top was totally collapsed by the roll and it had to just miss striking him on the head.

The vehicle's license plate number was recorded by the Patrol. Since it was registered in my name, the Patrol called me at my office the following Monday morning. I told them I would support them to charge Brian with reckless driving, which they did. I immediately suspended his driving for three months. When Brian appeared before the District Court, his attorney used his defense as the medication, Accutane, which he was taking for severe acne. The judge (who was John Paglia, my father's ex-attorney), enforced the three month suspension that I already had imposed on him an added a year's probation with a clean record or removal of his license for the year. Since his three month suspension was almost over, he was able to commence driving shortly after the hearing.

Since he had totaled the Tempo, he needed a new car. We ended up purchasing him a used Honda Prelude. Everything was fine for the next couple of years until he rear-ended another vehicle while entering Highway 16 coming home from school. The vehicle was still drivable so he drove it home. The rear-ender was Brian's fault and would have resulted in a year's suspension of his license. Since he rear-ended a Bellarmine parent who had just picked up her child, and caused minimal damage to her vehicle, we fixed both vehicles by me paying cash rather than reporting the accident. I rescued Brian from suffering the consequences of his mistake; normally not a good practice for a parent. However, I found myself doing it again later in Brian's life.

Although, the next two years at Hillhaven were stressful, because of our declining contribution to NME, we had become a close knit management team and were able to successfully tolerate the ever-increasing interference from NME management. One particular occasion of note will show the lunacy of Dick Eamer, NMEs lead cofounder, Chairman and CEO. Our senior management was frequently required to appear in front of Eamer and, his partner, Leonard Cohen, for financial reviews. On one occasion, our entire senior and regional operational management was summoned to the Board Room in the NME corporate office (about 30 of us in total). Mr. Eamer was very agitated over our performance and wanted to know what we were going to do about it. We had sent financial binders to him and others prior to our arrival, and when the meeting started, it was obvious Eamer was "loaded for bear."

In the middle of our opening remarks, he picked up our binders, threw them at us, swore at us, told us we were all fired and then stomped out of the room. We were torn between fear and absolute hilarity. We spent the remainder of the day sitting in the board room with NME management not knowing what was going to occur next. Although we had flown in the night before the meeting, we had scheduled an afternoon return flight, which we missed. Finally, our Group CEO, Bruce Busby, was called out of the room. After another couple of hours, Bruce returned and told us we were all rehired and that we could return home. Bruce, Bob Pacquer and I caught a taxi, headed to LAX, and through the taxi driver, were able to secure a reservation on a flight to Seattle. Eamer was a real loon.

Another incident of note occurred when a patient under our care died at one of our facilities in Wichita, Kansas. Investigation revealed that the patient was mistakenly given a chemical cleaner called Microquat. Apparently, one of the housekeeping staff had used a medicinal bottle to dispense the chemical and left it on the patient's bed side stand. The patient's nursing assistant erroneously concluded that the nurse had forgotten to give her the medicine so she gave it to the patient, killing her.

This event mushroomed into national news. CBS's 60 minutes contacted us for an interview. We reluctantly agreed. Knowing 60 minutes reputation for sensationalism, we hired Edelman Associates from Washington, DC, to train us on dealing with adverse communications. They determined I was the best on my feet at handling an adverse interview. Nonetheless, it was appropriate for the president to be interviewed so Marvin was appointed as the spokesperson.

Mike Wallace conducted the interview. Marvin sat at his desk dressed in a dark blue suit. Although the interview appeared to go reasonably well, when aired, 60 minutes used editing techniques to make Marvin appear as a greedy corporate criminal who could care less about our patients. That was in 1987. I haven't watched 60 minutes since (see Letter #2, section on the Media).

In the beginning of 1988, Marvin's two year agreement with NME as Hillhaven's President was going to expire. Although NME had an option to extend the agreement one year, they chose not to exercise the option. Alan Ewalt, the NME VP of Human Resources called me and asked my advice on how to recruit Marvin's replacement. I suggested that our industry needed new blood and that it might make sense to recruit someone from the hospitality industry rather than hire another healthcare manager. Al passed this onto Eamer and he bought it, and hired his friend, Lester Korn (Korn/Ferry International) to conduct the search.

"Brilliant career move coming up!"

At the same time as the search began, Bruce Busby took a position in LA reporting directly to Eamer. He would head up a "New Business Venture Group." Bruce and I had become pretty good friends and I hated to see him go, but it appeared to be a good opportunity for him and NME had presumably determined the new president would take over both the role of CEO of the Long Term Care Group and President of Hillhaven.

A couple months went by. We all wondered who our new boss would be. One day, Bruce called me from LA and said that Eamer had selected a potential candidate; he wanted Bruce to fly up to Seattle for one final interview before making the offer. Bruce and the candidate met at the airport for the interview. Afterwards, he called me to tell me, "The guy fits Eamer's image; he was VP Operations for Westin Hotels based in Seattle. He wants to come down to meet management before accepting the offer." Bruce would have him contact me for the introduction.

The candidate's name was Chris Marker. We talked by phone and made arrangements for him to meet in my office to introduce him to Hillhaven. After my meeting with Marker, Bruce called and asked me what I thought. I said, "He seems ok." Inside, I was a little nervous about him because he seemed so formal in both his speech and dress, but I remembered my comment to Al Ewalt that we could probably stand some new blood in the industry.

This was in late February or March 1988. On April 1, Chris Marker started as President of Hillhaven (Eamer did not give him title as CEO, pending a review of his initial performance). Marvin was still on the scene as lame duck President, to help break in Marker. Marker barely tolerated this; he wanted Marvin out of the picture as quickly as possible. He was upset that he agreed to a salary lower than Marvin's. Because of this, I talked to Marvin about leaving early which he did after cutting a final retirement package with NME.

By mid-May, 1988, the era of Chris Marker was underway. He formed a formal executive committee that was to meet weekly; he required all managers to wear coat and tie whenever traveling, even on weekends. He came to my office one day and asked me how best to sign his name; Chris, Christopher, Chris Marker, Mr. Marker, etc. I was at lost for words; thinking what difference does it make, I took the political route and told him I thought "Chris" was fine.

Chris and I did not hit it off. Since Chris was never honest with me, I can only speculate on a few possible reasons:
- I was too close to Hillhaven employees and probably had the best rapport with all levels of management and staff. Chris wanted to become that.
- I liked an informal management style that was results-oriented; Marker liked a much more formal organization.

- I thought his decision-making ability was severely lacking in that he almost never made a decision on his own, even when it was necessary.
- I was looking for a Human Resources Director and he "suggested" I interview someone at Westin that he used to work with. Although I did interview the person, I hired someone else. As it turned out, although he never ordered me to hire the person, in retrospect, he considered his request more than a suggestion.

Here is a summary of events that occurred over the 18 months that I lasted while working for him:
- He actually tried to belittle me when he said that I seemed like a kid from the small town of Tacoma who hadn't had that much exposure.
- At a Risk Management meeting at NME headquarters, I had flown down the night before the meeting. I had dinner with Bruce Busby and his wife, Cindy. Bruce asked me how Marker was doing. I said, "Good. He is looking at hiring a marketing VP, which I think makes sense." The next day, apparently while on a break from the meeting, Bruce mentioned to Chris what I had said regarding his hiring a Marketing VP. After the meeting, in the car on the way to LAX, Chris confronted me and said he did not appreciate my discussion with Bruce regarding hiring a Marketing VP and that things discussed in the Executive Committee needed to stay in the Executive Committee.
- He asked me to interview his candidate, Ron Olsted, from Westin Hotels. I met Ron at the Black Angus in Federal Way, Washington. Ron naturally asked me many questions regarding salary and benefits and, without committing to anything, I gave him a general overview of our structure. When this got back to Chris, he was incensed and told me that I shouldn't have done that. I never did understand why

he had me interview Ron in the first place if I couldn't respond to his questions.
- Once again, Chris met with me to suggest that I should find a job in Tacoma; he commented that my father was well known and I should have no trouble securing local employment. I told him I liked my career here (political response, I know) and would like to stay.
- We held Regional meetings in Virginia Beach and Arizona. Chris saw how I seemed totally at ease with the audiences both in formal presentations and at the evening cocktail parties. I don't believe he took kindly to this.
- Knowing my future was in trouble, in about September, 1989, I had a meeting with Chris and asked him directly if I had a career here. His response (this is a direct quote), "Probably not for 30 years but for at least five." With that, even though he was not my kind of manager, due to my many personal commitments, he alleviated my concerns. I said that was fine with me.

About one month later, I set up a meeting in Chris's office to discuss the process of finding a replacement for Frank Kabisch, the HR Director I had hired, who turned out not to be a good fit for the role. The meeting was set for 11 AM. Upon closing the door for what I thought was my meeting, Chris stopped me cold. He said, "We've decided to make a change." I said, "What kind of a change?" He said, "You!"

Completely lost for words, I just sat there silently. I finally asked him "Why?" His reply, "You're not qualified!" Stunned, I couldn't believe my ears. Chris went on to say that they were eliminating my position (a flat out lie to protect both his personal ass and corporate liability). He stated there was a representative from an outplacement firm they had hired waiting for me in the lobby of the Sheraton Hotel across the street. I could evaluate them and use them or take $15,000, my choice. I did not want to go over, but he made it clear if I didn't he would consider it an act of insubordination. So after asking him who knew about my termination, I quietly left.

I went across the street to the Sheraton where a representative from Lee, Hecht, Harrison was waiting, and, after a brief discussion, decided to use them. After Marker explained the Company's settlement offer, which, of course, was sub-standard for someone with my history, I asked to fly to LA to meet with Leonard Cohen, NME's Vice Chairman, which was granted me.

I arrived at home about 2PM. Sandy was in the backyard when I arrived. She asked me what I was doing home so early. I responded that I just got fired from Hillhaven. She said that it couldn't be; that I was Mr. Hillhaven. I said, "Not anymore!"

I flew to LA a few days later to discuss the terms of my departure with Leonard. I'm sure Cohen and Marker had a discussion about my terms before I arrived, but in any event, Leonard actually set the financial terms of the settlement, which were generous. I flew back to Seattle only to find out that I was to negotiate the language of the settlement with Rich Adcock, our counsel, who we had promoted from NME's legal staff a couple years before. I cut the deal and left Hillhaven after about 13 ½ years; 48 years old and unemployed.

So ended my relationship with Chris Marker! Marker was the type of person that I have always tried to avoid, but obviously could not due to my career. He was concerned more about his image then getting the job done. He was an "empty suit, all show and no go." Important things to him were how well he was dressed; how his hair was combed; how he signed his name; never chew gum (no kidding, he actually told me that once); and never send cards out with a printed signature. I despised him for many years after I departed Hillhaven.

He also ended up firing Dan Mosca, who knew more about operations than virtually anyone in our Company. In a nutshell, the hiring of Marker was not only my waterloo but a mistake for Hillhaven. Finally, Eamer figured that out. He moved Bruce Busby back as CEO with instructions to fix the problem. I was delighted. I thought for sure he would fire Marker. He never did, although he moved him to the side so he had no real responsibility. I never understood why Bruce kept him. I can only presume that it was because Eamer hired him and he didn't want to "rock the boat." Anyway, the company was sold in 1996 and my understanding was that Marker received $12 million with the sale.

"Real justice in play here!"

Chris Marker target, given to me at Christmas

1990-1993

The next three years or so were to be one the roughest, most unsettling periods of my life, including the period when I was going through a divorce. Lee Hecht Harrison was based in Bellevue. I commuted from Gig Harbor, although not every day. There were a lot of supposedly growth-building exercises, but it became very difficult for an ex-senior vice president to find a job, any job for that matter. My self-worth became a big problem for me.

At home, I was a mess. Sandy had all she could do to put up with my hate of Marker and my constant anger. It came close to costing me my marriage. Sandy was a jewel for the most part during this period, but one person can only put up with so much. Through thick and thin (and there was a lot of thin), our marriage survived.

"Am I fortunate!"

Searching for a new career, I found I needed to market my skills and not my title (which, if used, would result in an immediate rejection). My experience with this firm was less than satisfying so I stopped using it. I joined a grass roots group called Forty Plus, also based in Bellevue that I found much more to my liking. They were people just like me, all unemployed, at all levels of professional and executive management who helped each other. I found that, because of my background, I could make a considerable contribution to others. This helped me to rekindle my self-worth.

Since I had a severance package that included 15 months' salary and continued benefits, I decided to start a labor relations consulting and training business. After working at new business development for about a year (until about January, 1991), I still hadn't developed any real client base. I joined Connelly and Associates, a labor relations consulting firm based in Lakewood, Washington. Jack Connelly was extremely gracious to provide me with office space and only required that I reimburse him when I started making money. I tried hard but could not develop enough of a clientele base to support our family or satisfy Jack's expectations so, after less than a year with Jack, and my severance package due to expire. I decided to try another approach.

I learned that because of my Psychology degree received in 1965, I could qualify as a vocational rehabilitation consultant (God bless our government; only a degree in psychology mattered albeit 25 years old and never used). I got my rehab license.

In late spring, 1992, with my severance package expired, I took a consulting position with Federal Way-based Whittall Associates. They did general human resources consulting and had a contract with the State to provide vocational rehabilitation. I had known Pete

Whittall as the Director of Compensation at Weyerhaeuser, so I was easily able to see him. Pete hired me and said I could probably make up to $75,000 per year (about 1/3 of my annual salary at Hillhaven; beggars can't be choosy; I needed to support my family).

My direct supervisor was a lady named Kathleen. Kathleen was a terrible supervisor. She had been an administrator at the University of Puget Sound, and had little or no experience supervising employees in the business world. Given my background, it was very hard to tolerate her. Nevertheless, I had to for the time being. She was my boss.

"Damn it!"

Although I did make some money with Whittall, as with Connelly Associates, it was not enough to support my family and I hated reporting to Kathleen. I even tried to convince Pete to have me work independently. Rightfully so, he said no. So, frustrated, I quit and began collecting unemployment compensation.

"The height of humiliation!"

During the last three years, I went from a senior officer of a large healthcare company, making a large salary, with, what I thought, was a secure position, to becoming one of the mass of unemployed, with a heavy financial burden on my back. Lesson: don't ever take your life's position for granted. Shit happens to all of us and, when it does, it's not what has happened so much as how one deals with it. And, as those close to me knew, emotionally, I was not doing well. Even murder (of Marker) and suicide occasionally popped into my mind. But I put those thoughts aside; I knew that the only way to come back was to persevere.

"Great thinking!"

During this period, Tina had begun high school at Puyallup High. Besides being a good student, she was also a very talented actress. She acted in virtually every play, sometimes taking the leading role. She developed a very close relationship with another talented actress and singer, Bonnie Strader. Tina and Bonnie had been close friends since grade school; Bonnie developed a brain tumor at this tender age and although she survived it then, it eventually took her as a young adult.

As a junior, Tina and a football player were caught smoking pot during a weekend outing with several other students. Linda Quinn, the Principal, suspended Tina for five days and prohibited her participation in two future plays. Not so for the football athlete. Although he was suspended briefly, he was permitted to participate in all games.

"Congratulations Ms. Quinn; another example of equal justice!"

During November, 1991, my father underwent surgery to repair an aortic aneurysm. Although the surgery was voluntary, the doctors determined he was living with a time bomb because the aneurysm was growing. We knew it was risky since Dad was 79 and not in good health. He made it through the surgery, but unfortunately, died of a pulmonary embolism suffered as a result of the surgery three days later. His funeral brought an overflow crowd at St. Charles Borromeo Catholic Church. Dad was very well liked.

I gave the eulogy. With his draped coffin in front of me, I started it with, "There lies a big man"! It was meant to have a double meaning; Dad was physically large and, as I continued the eulogy, I stated he was 16 pounds at birth and had an equally large (kind) heart. This was one of the best speeches of my life. I was proud to have done that for Dad. He and I were very close so his death was difficult for me. Being the oldest child, I also needed to help Mom with all the arrangements and estate issues.

On top of the normal trauma, we were forced to deal with another haunting issue. While Dad was alive, my brother, Danny, had been indicted for embezzlement and opening a bank account in his employer's name without the authority to do so (Federal crime). Danny had been a problem for my folks since he was 14, the year our brother, Gary, was killed. Unfortunately, Dad had solved the loss of Gary by completely spoiling Danny. Consequently, Danny never had to fend for himself. He became a wheeler dealer, a proverbial liar, and a burden to the folks. Dad kept bailing Danny out of trouble. He even blamed Danny's employer for not catching him sooner, thus limiting their monetary liability. This was hanging over Dad at the time of his surgery; I really believe Dad knew he was largely responsible for Danny's plight and very risky surgery was his way out.

After Dad's death, Mom became aware of what I intuitively knew all along; Dad had been funneling money to Danny for many years so he could live a life style completely beyond his means. The Federal prosecutors were trying to somehow tie the family into the scheme. Consequently, Mom had to undergo several depositions. This ended up being a terribly emotional and humiliating time for her. Danny remained free while the investigation continued. Subsequently, he appeared before Jack Tanner, a Federal judge for this district, and was sentenced to five years in prison (of which two were probation). I remember the wailing of his three daughters in the courtroom as he was led away.

Brian graduated from Bellarmine in May 1990 culminating a unique Ruffo history of Papa Frank graduating in 1930, me in 1960, and Brian in 1990 — all 30 years apart. Brian decided to attend the University of Portland. During the summers, he worked at Wild Waves Amusement Park in Federal Way. Sandy was still in school. While in school, she worked part time in Long Term Care. She received her RN degree in 1992 from Pacific Lutheran University and landed a full time job with a newly constructed nursing facility in Gig Harbor.

Sandy graduating from Pacific Lutheran University, 1992
I'm greeting Sandy as she receives her diploma

Brian decided to major in engineering and room with Luke Xitco, his high school buddy. Here was a disaster in the making. Brian's grades were miserable. Besides that, sometime during the school year, Brian and others organized a dorm party, hired strippers and charged a $5 admission. Bad news! Thinking the event would be kept from school administration, they held it without fear. Big mistake; somebody ratted on them.

The school got us involved; suspended Brian; then let him back in with the proviso that he view several movies on sexual deviant behavior. We went along with the punishment, but my view was it was a waste of Brian's time and my money to continue at Portland U. So the next quarter, he transferred to Pierce College, a local Community College. After finishing up at Pierce College, he decided to attend Central Washington University's flight school. Brian liked both Pierce College and Central. He made some lifelong friends at both places.

One day in the winter of 1993-94, I got a call from Brian, sobbing and generally upset. We had traded his Honda Prelude in for a new Daihatsu, four wheeler, which presumably would be great for the snowy country of Ellensburg in Eastern Washington. On a beautiful winter day, he had decided to travel "off road" solo into the mountains. Unfortunately, he got lost and found himself in an area where the Daihatsu ended up on its side. Alone and unable to move the vehicle, he had decided to attempt to walk out. Making it to the Yakima River, he used two road flares and finally attracted the attention of bystanders on the other side of the river who saw the flares. They convinced Brian to cross the icy river. As soon as he crossed, they put him in their car and took him to a local nurse's house, who warmed him up by placing him in a tepid bath. Saved to live another day! I had to hire a tow truck with four-wheel drive, chains, and crane to retrieve the vehicle.

"Another $500!"

Of course, after paying for many hours of flying time, during Brian's last quarter, he decided to change his major to aviation computer science, and graduated in June, 1995. This was a smart move due to developing high blood pressure (a family trait), and, with a few bumps, he has thus far had a very successful career.

"Whew!"

Since I first departed Hillhaven, I stayed in close touch with Dan Baty. Dan had formed Columbia Pacific, a management consulting firm that focused on investing in retirement housing facilities. While he was still at Hillhaven, he had partnered with a contractor, Bill Colson, who he knew from the nursing home days, to form Holiday Retirement. He also had purchased Columbia Winery and was building quite a thriving business.

During the summer of 1992, while departing for our summer boat cruise, Dan Baty's secretary, Mary Kirk, called me on my cell (yes, cell phones were just being introduced to the mass market) to inform me that Dan wanted to have a discussion with me. He and Bill

Colson were in the process of purchasing a mortgage pool from the Resolution Trust Corporation (RTC) and Dan thought I would be a good fit to inspect the nursing and retirement home assets behind each mortgage.

Sensing a real opportunity, I asked Dan if I should turn the boat around. He said no but come by and see him when I returned home, which was to be in about two weeks. When we returned, I met Dan in his office. His office was a converted condominium adjacent to railroad tracks facing the waterfront in Old Tacoma. In addition to Mary Kirk, Dan had hired Ray Brandstrom and Chuck Uhlman, ex-Hillhaven employees. Ray ran the winery and helped Dan in financial matters and Chuck was a project manager for new facility construction.

After a brief explanation on the $203 million Real Estate Mortgage Investment Conduit (REMIC) that he and Colson were about to invest in, Dan gave me his vision of my job. It would be to ride herd on 60 nursing homes and retirement housing facilities to be sure they would continue to perform and make monthly mortgage payments. He would pay me $50,000 annual salary. I accepted and started on November 1, 1992, almost three years after leaving Hillhaven. Not knowing at the time, this was to be the beginning of a career that would provide tremendous growth opportunity eventually culminating in my retirement in July 2007.

We formed a separate company, called Somerset Management (name courtesy of wife, Sandy) to act as "Special Industry Servicer" for managing the pool assets. Dan and I flew to New York and met with officials of Daiwa Bank, who financed most of the deal. Their offices were in the World Trade Center (whoever thought that less than 10 years later, these buildings would come down, killing almost 3,000 Americans). Here was a guy with little or no financial experience directly involved in 202 million dollar deal. Dan said "no big deal; you'll do fine!"

"Scary."

One morning, Daiwa called our office to set up a conference call. Its purpose—what financial barometer we were going to use for interest, US Treasury or LIBOR. They wanted our opinion that day. Holy crap! Dan and Ray were on vacation, both in Europe, and unreachable. I had never heard of LIBOR. I stalled them until later in the day; they said fine but they needed to know today.

Panicked, I jumped in my car; headed to the nearest Borders Books and bought a large financial book called "Barron's". Back at the office, I studied the chapter on LIBOR (London Interbank Offered Rate) vs. US Treasury and determined LIBOR fluctuated daily and was more international in scope. Voila! That had to be the one. The conference call occurred about 6PM Eastern Time and I said we recommend LIBOR. With little fanfare, everyone was in agreement.

"Such brilliance!"

Managing Somerset required a lot of travel. I found it to be both challenging and fun; and I learned a ton. Somerset was only the beginning. Having a great combination of business smarts, risk-taking ability, and shooting for longer term success, Dan would create more opportunities.

In late 1992, beginning of 1993, an older retirement home in Renton, Washington, was bankrupt. We made a bid on it and got it. The three of us (Dan, Ray, and me) talked about what we should do with it now; we had heard about this new concept of Assisted Living. On the spot, we decided to give it a try. Why not; US population was aging, we all had considerable experience in senior housing/healthcare, it was a new industry, and government involvement was almost non-existent.

We decided I would learn all I could about Assisted Living. I joined a new National Assisted Living organization based in DC, and attended their next regular meeting. We put $250,000 in improvements in the building and started marketing it as Assisted Living. Dan put Ray and me in charge of operations.

About the same time we got wind of a building being built in Everett, Washington. It was a 75-25% partnership. The 75% piece wanted out. We bought his position; hired the 25% partner as managers (a couple); completed construction, and opened the facility.

Our occupancy went over 90% in both buildings in about eight months. We had something going! In July, 1993, with Dan as CEO, Ray as President, and me, as Executive Vice President, we incorporated the new company in the State of Washington as Assisted Living of America (ALA).

"Real creative!"

1994-1999

Our company was off and running. In order to build bulk, we began acquiring older buildings for renovation. More office staff was required. By 1994, we had grown to about 25 buildings. We were outgrowing the little condo office in Tacoma. Because Hillhaven was in the Tacoma labor market, in October, 1994, we moved the company to Seattle. This was not to my liking. Sandy and I had just sold our Horsehead Bay Drive home and were in the process of building a new home within the Gig Harbor City limits. I made the decision to commute, which I did for the next 13 years.

Our Gig Harbor home

Since Ray and I had little operational background, we knew it was time to hire someone to run the operations. This became a challenge. In fact, although we grew to almost a billion dollar company by the time I retired, we never were totally successful in building a great operational team that worked well with the corporate office. And since we needed operations, whenever there was an issue between operations and the Seattle office, Dan generally felt compelled to side with operations, no matter what the issue.

During summer of 1995, we received a large (for us) private capital investment from Japan-based Sanyo Electric. We expanded into new construction by designing three prototypes, and embarked on a building program.

Ray and me, first groundbreaking, Kirkland Lodge, 1994

As he did at Hillhaven, Dan was doing his thing, and doing it fast; it was Ray's and my job to keep up and it was sometimes challenging. We planned on going public to raise more capital for expansion. Knowing we were going public, we held an employee contest to change our name from Assisted Living of America. Ray and I picked the winner from several entrants (Dan could care less). "Emeritus" won (which meant "retired with dignity/honor"). In November, 1995, we came out with our Initial Public Offering (IPO) at $15 per share.

My daughter Tina graduated from Puyallup High School in June, 1995. During her senior year, I took her to several university campuses, including Willamette, Santa Clara, Stanford, and Claremont. She had done extremely well on her SAT. With a high school GPA of about 3.8, she was accepted to all (except Stanford, due to the liberal "affirmative action" approach that many "elitist" schools used). She chose Claremont. This worked out well for me since I frequently made business trips to Southern California; I was able to visit often. I was shocked on my first visit to see my beautiful daughter with orange hair.

"Welcome Dad!"

Tina at Claremont with her "new look"

Tina did very well at Claremont, graduating cum laude with a double major in History and Economics. She did play rugby and received a slight concussion as a result. Her rugby days were over after the injury. Her junior year, she went to Victoria College in Wellington, New Zealand. When she arrived, we received a disturbing message from our local sheriff; they had received word Tina was missing in the mountains of New Zealand with another classmate. Apparently, the college held an outing for the new arrivals. Tina (and her new found friend, Gail Winter) had drifted away from the group. Realizing they were lost, and that August in New Zealand was winter, they spent the night under an evergreen tree covering themselves with boughs to stay warm.

We were in total panic. I was starting to make plans to fly to New Zealand when we received another call from the sheriff; they had been found! They were rescued by helicopter, and, of course, made the front page of the New Zealand newspapers.

"Aren't children fun to raise; especially when they are adventuresome!"

Tina and Gail, "hiking" in New Zealand mountains

Emeritus was continuing to grow. Internationally, I was put in charge of forming a joint venture with Sanyo Electric to start retirement housing in Japan. I would be spending the next six years traveling to Japan to put the venture together and, ultimately, completing construction of our first (and, as it turned out, only) building. After several months of negotiation, we formed Sanyo Emeritus, a Japanese company, with me as Executive Vice President.

Dan Baty, Satoshi Iue (Chairman of Sanyo Electric Ltd.) and me, 1996

Emeritus-Sanyo Senior management 1996

Forming Sanyo-Emeritus partnership 1997

Sanyo- Emeritus: Kurashiki, Japan

Me and Ray Brandstrom dedicating the building, 2000

Domestically, our corporate staff had grown out of our facilities next to the famous Pike Place Market. I found a larger building which we moved into in 1996. Today, this location continues to be our corporate office. Having been through three tries at hiring operational management, Dan apparently decided that Ray and I were the problem. No doubt, he came to this conclusion with the help of the existing operational and financial management, who made us political scapegoats. Both Ray and I agreed, one gal in particular (her name was Sara Curtis) played an instrumental role in undermining us. Because we had so many vested interests in the company and because we were powerless to do otherwise, both of us stepped away from day-to day management with little fanfare. I kept responsibility for Japan and that was it. Although at the time it appeared to be another career set back, it was not to be the case. In fact, because of my lengthy involvement settling the family estate, it turned out to be fortuitous.

"Gulp!"

I now had spare time to fill. I had always wanted the opportunity to try public service. So I ran for, and was elected to the Gig Harbor City Council. I filled a two year term created as a result of expanding the Council from five to seven members. I was then re-elected to a second four year term.

Me running for Gig Harbor City Council

Campaigning was a real pain. We did the usual—we participated in debates sponsored by the local newspaper or service organizations. We put up campaign signs. We went door-to-door. My opponents for both terms were a husband and wife team who ran a local retail business. The first term, I ran against the wife; second term, against the husband. On weekends, most of our campaign signs were knocked down, presumably by kids. Sandy and I would patrol them, particularly on Saturday and Sunday mornings.

One weekend, we got up very early and repaired or replaced all my downed signs. That Saturday night, I received a call from my opponent (the husband), who had seen my signs up and all his down later that morning. Being an ex-Naval Officer, like me, he accused me of being the "Viet Cong" (reference to our enemy in South Vietnam). I did not take kindly to that. I said nothing publically but called him on it privately. I don't think he ever believed I had nothing to do with his downed signs.

"C'est la vie!"

I found being on the Council personally challenging. I was used to quickly identifying issues, debating them in a small group, and then making a decision. Not so in politics. The process is bureaucratic and very cumbersome. I found several Council colleagues to be more interested in their own agenda rather than doing what was in the best interest of Gig Harbor (not true for all). Over my six years as a council member, I became increasingly frustrated. Being a private property rights advocate, I saw a microcosm of the continual eroding of these rights throughout our country on a much broader scale (see Letter #2). I chose not to run again; my term expired December 31, 2005.

Frank Ruffo not seeking re-election in fall

Council member cites commitments to new job as reason

CALLIE WHITE
of the Gateway

Monday night at the Gig Harbor City Council, Council member Frank Ruffo announced his intention to not run for a third term on the council.

Ruffo cited work as his reason for vacating his position.

"I have made this decision because I resumed duties as an officer of Emeritus Assisted Living and, because of travel and other commitments with our company, don't feel I have ample time to devote to the council," Ruffo wrote in a letter to Mayor Gretchen Wilbert and distributed to other council members. Additionally, Ruffo indicated that his schedule for the rest of his term will likely keep him away from "some meetings between now and December."

Ruffo has been on the council for about six years, and has served on the city's parks committee.

During Ruffo's tenure, the city saw a major expansion in its park spaces. Wilkenson Farm, Skansie Brothers and Eddon Boatyard are three of the properties acquired by the city in that time.

Ruffo was also the council's representative in negotiations for purchase Eddon Boatyard; the purchase was widely heralded as a success by community members and city staffers because the purchase price includes a guarantee that the former owners of the site will be responsible for all environmental cleanup.

Ruffo counts Eddon Boatyard as perhaps his most significant achievement during his membership on the council.

"We did a lot," Ruffo said. Ruffo's spot will not be the only one up for grabs. Council members John Picinich, Steve Ekberg and Derek Young all share terms that will expire in November. So far, only Picinich and Young have expressed their intention to run in September. The deadline to file for a candidacy in July 31.

Reach reporter Callie White at 853-9224 or by e-mail at callie.white@gateline.com.

Peninsula Gateway, April 2005

My brother Danny was released from prison after 30 months, being allowed to serve the rest of his five years on probation. He made a pitch to Mom to reopen the King's Drive-In. Our family had owned the real estate but never ran the operations. Mom agreed to form a 50-50 partnership (luckily, she never signed any partnership papers). Danny borrowed a large sum of money from one of his friends for improvements, hired his daughters to help, and opened the business. I was proud of him; maybe he was finally turning his life around.

One day, Danny called me to ask my help with Mom. He claimed she was hanging out at the drive-in daily, interfering and disrupting the business. Knowing Mom's propensity to do this, I set up a meeting at the drive-in. I tried to get them to draw up partnership papers clearly outlining who the operating manager would be. Although Mom agreed Danny was in charge of operations, she made it clear that the building was hers and she expected rent (Danny was already in arrears). She would contact our family attorney to draw up an agreement (luckily, she never did; by not forming a partnership, she and her estate avoided liability for the cost of the improvements). I then adjourned the meeting.

In September, 1999, Mom had a very bad tread mill test. She was diagnosed with severe heart disease and immediately hospitalized. A heart surgeon was called in and, after consultation, he told me that her only chance was by-pass surgery; without it she would die inside two months. The surgery would be "no cakewalk". Mom decided to have the surgery. On September 3, as Danny and I walked alongside each side of the gurney as she was being wheeled into the operating room, she stated, "You boys get along!" The medical staff wheeled her through the double doors into surgery. She died on the operating table.

Mom had long ago rekindled her relationship with the Church and was very active at St. Charles Parish in Tacoma. Her funeral was very well attended. Although I loved Mom, because of the cantankerous relationship we had, I could not find it in myself to give her eulogy. So I asked my good friend, Mike O'Brien, who, when we were kids, had developed a fond relationship with Mom, to deliver it. Mike graciously said yes, and delivered a beautiful memory of us kids growing up as part of Mom's household.

After her funeral, I found out that brother Danny was telling everyone that he was "rich". In fact, because of providing him with lifelong support and having reached the conclusion he didn't know how to handle money, Dad and Mom had excluded him from the will. As executor of the family estate, I knew this; Mom and Dad wanted to be sure Danny's three daughters would be receiving what Danny thought was his when each turned 25.

When Danny found this out, he was not a happy camper. He had told his friend who advanced the funds for the drive-in improvements that he would be paid from his share of the Estate. With no money, he hired an attorney to explore contesting the will. He had no basis for doing so. Danny had tried to do two things: turn his daughters against me, and put a guilt trip on them that the money was rightfully his. He failed in both cases.

Within the year, Danny was arrested by authorities for violating his parole. Among other violations, he affiliated with an ex-con which was prohibited. Appearing before Judge Tanner (the same judge who sentenced him earlier), he was incarcerated for the rest of his sentence, another thirty months. The drive-in was closed. Danny's friend came to me for payment of the funds. Since the estate was not accountable for the debt, there was no way I could authorize payment, and I wasn't about to accept it personally. Unbeknownst to me at the time, I would spend the next three years settling the estate, largely because of the commercial property and the ensuing environmental issues (see Letter #2).

The year 1999 found the Assisted Living industry in dire straits. Many construction types had entered the game thinking it was a way to make a quick buck. Unfortunately, the majority had no operational experience. Consequently, the industry had become overbuilt. In addition, the economy at large was crashing because the hi-tech industry had done exactly the same thing.

Emeritus stock plummeted to under $1.00 per share. I had decided I was likely going to have to work the rest of my life since my financial well-being was tied mostly to the company. At Emeritus, as with every institution in the industrialized world, we were very concerned about the impact of Y2K (the year 2000 impact on all our systems which turned out to be a big farce). It was during this year that I began to come back to Emeritus full time. Ray had already come back as CFO due to the young CFO Dan had promoted reporting misleading numbers to the financial markets. I returned as coordinator between us and a Portland-based company facing bankruptcy we had agreed to manage. And luckily, Sara Curtis, who had previously undermined Ray and I, had involuntarily departed.

"Ah, justice returns!"

2000-2007

In November, 2003, Gary Becker, the senior operations guru had decided to fire his Vice President of Human Resources. Although I viewed this as a mistake (she was a sharp gal, but did not march to the operational drum that had been in place for several years), I went along with it (for political reasons), helped terminate her and wrote her termination agreement. I still regard her highly today and, without her knowledge, recommended her for an HR position.

"Isn't corporate life wonderful?!"

Guess who was going to fill the HR void? Me. But what I consider the soft side of HR not being my bag, I promoted a new HR manager from within; I took over Risk Management, Purchasing, and

Nurse Consulting. As a consultant myself, I now had major management responsibilities with no official title. No big deal since I was not into titles, but because I was not an officer, I had no Directors and Officers liability coverage which left me open for considerable exposure. I asked Dan about becoming an officer again for protection and he thought it was a good idea.

"Back in the fold again!"

Emeritus Management, Scottsdale, AZ.

Seeing the overbuilt nature of the industry, we had shut down our construction arm early on. That was instrumental in saving us from the fate of many others. Also, due to Dan's ability to take over assets and either lease them to Emeritus or have us manage them, we avoided having to take a significant hit on our books. Although we had outside investors that required we achieve certain covenants, when we didn't, we were able to develop a plan to alleviate their concerns.

That said, 2000 to 2004 were tough years for our industry and our Company. And, although we had some okay operational types, we had no crackerjacks as leaders. In fact, operational management was a "good old boy" network akin to a secret brotherhood that demanded utmost loyalty. Consequently, I frequently found myself in a quandary caught between operations and finance. In fact our operational leadership was marginal, and although Ray and I wanted to make a change, Dan didn't want to rock the boat. Anyway, the best the operational team could do was to stop the bleeding. During this period, we faced "delisting" of our stock several times.

We again embarked on an acquisition mode. One of our major competitors (Alterra) based out of Milwaukee had gone bankrupt and we made a bid to acquire them. I was in charge of the acquisition team. After several months of meetings, their management found another suitor (Brookdale Senior Living) to protect their jobs and we were eliminated as contenders.

In 2005, the economy began to roll; we had shifted from the American Stock Exchange to the New York (the Big Board). Although we had lost a major resident care law suit in Texas (we fired the VP in charge as a result; he should have been fired long ago), investors started to take notice of the industry. In spite of our mediocre operational performance, largely because of the strategic decisions Dan made and Ray's financial advice, our reputation began to grow. Our stock price began to rise. Everything was looking up.

On August 29, 2005, Hurricane Katrina slammed into the Gulf Coast, devastating New Orleans and Southern Mississippi. Our recently-opened building in Biloxi was destroyed. Fortunately, we evacuated the residents so there were no injuries.

Unbelievably, less than a month later, Hurricane Rita set its aim towards the East Coast of Texas. We had three facilities in harm's way so Ray and I set up a "war room" in the Seattle office. With me in charge, we prepared for the worst; I chartered a Boeing 757 to evacuate all our residents to our large building in Dallas (I put the $60,000.00 airplane charge on my American Express card— by far the largest credit card charge I ever made). Unfortunately, the Federal Government closed all airports so we had to bus our residents to Dallas. When the Hurricane hit on September 24, 2005, we had safely evacuated all three buildings.

I felt good about our handling of these crises, and was extremely proud of our staff at all levels, but particularly those on the "front line".

Me with Emeritus HR staff, Assaggio Restaurant, 2005

LETTERS TO MY CHILDREN

Hurricane Katrina also touches our small town

SCOOP du jour
George Le Masurier

FRANK Ruffo did not watch the devastation of New Orleans on television. He did not see, as most other Americans did, the images of fear-stricken people marooned on their rooftops, or the blurry scenes of deadly winds and water raging through the cities of the Gulf Coast.

By the time Hurricane Katrina hit land on Monday, Aug. 29, unleashing one of the worst natural disasters in America's history, Ruffo was already dog-tired from more than 24 hours of non-stop crisis management. He was busy trying to save the lives of 100-plus elderly people in his care and his scores of employees, and working out the logistics of food, fuel, power and water like a general in some faraway war-torn place.

Ruffo, the amiable Gig Harbor City Council member, began his marathon early Sunday morning when it became certain that Katrina would smash into the Mississippi and Louisiana coastlines. He's one of three co-founders and the vice-president of Emeritus, the second-largest operator of assisted living facilities in America. He runs 183 facilities housing 15,000 units in 33 states, four of them in upper Mississippi – and one in Biloxi.

They began evacuating everyone from the 190-unit Biloxi facility to other Emeritus facilities in Hattiesburg, about 40 miles north of the coast and to other sites in Louisiana, despite the known risk that 2-3 percent of residents do not survive the trauma of such a move.

As the storm hit, Hattiesburg also lost power and ran out of fuel for its generator. They had no potable water. They commandeered a Trailways bus and with several vans moved the elderly residents a second time to Texas and other safer places. His employees often had to wait six to eight hours in lines at the few remaining open gas stations.

With telephone lines down, Ruffo could only communicate by cell phones from his corporate office in Seattle, and later in the week as he worked from the Emeritus regional headquarters in Texas.

After the storm had passed and the extent of the wreckage began to sink in, Ruffo is now coping with the aftermath. The $8 million Biloxi building is missing its roof and suffered excessive water damage. But that's the least of his problems.

He has 14 employees still missing. Almost all of the Biloxi workers and many of the Hattiesburg employees are now homeless, many living at the assisted living facilities because they have nowhere else to go.

The frontline employees became so exhausted that she flew in nurses from Emeritus homes in Florida to give them a break. His managers are handing out cash so employees can purchase basic necessities. ATMs and many banks no longer exist. He's positioned one employee inside one of the few functioning banks handing out cash instead of pay-roll checks, knowing that he'll be facing an accounting horror somewhere up the road.

Ruffo is busied himself, but he's flying down to Mississippi next week to work hands-on and thank his employees who kept everyone safe. They defied the statistics by not losing a single resident.

This presents a stark contrast to reports of some nursing homes in New Orleans where staff simply abandoned the facilities, leaving its inhabitants to die.

He can't help thinking that his company is just one of thousands of businesses in the Gulf Coast struggling to survive and trying to continue serving its customers so they, too, can survive.

When simply everything is gone, he says, is nearly unfathomable to figure out how to keep operating without the simple structures of society that we normally take for granted.

About Frank Ruffo
- Served on City Council since 2001. Stepping down this year.
- Co-founded Emeritus in July 1993 and took it public in December 1995.
- Went to high school with Emeritus CEO and co-founder Dan Baty and worked with him at the now defunct Hillhaven nursing homes headquartered in Tacoma.
- Worked at Weyerhaeuser before going to Hillhaven.
- Now oversees the administration of Emeritus.
- The company has 8,500 employees.

Peninsula Gateway article on me, September 14, 2005

During the spring of 2006, I injured myself while working on "*Island Mist* II", a 52 foot Bayliner we purchased in 2004. The engine room hatch fell, striking my head. Thinking nothing of it at the time, I started experiencing severe headaches. By mid-June, I had constant head and neck soreness, and finally started to lose feeling on the left side of my body. After having an MRI, my doctor called me immediately to tell me to get to a hospital; I had a life-threatening bi-lateral (both sides) subdural hematoma.

Island Mist (II), 2004-2008

After the surgery, I spent the rest of the summer recuperating at home. I had experienced another life-threatening event about two years before and, I started giving retirement considerable thought. With some encouragement from both my wife, Sandy, (who had retired a year earlier) and friends, I made the decision to retire. I returned to work after Labor Day; met with Dan and we agreed that I would work to the end of the year and officially retire on July 1, 2007, the month following my 65th birthday.

From a financial perspective, the timing was perfect. Our stock continued to rise, and after satisfying all legal requirements for no longer being considered an insider, I was able to solidify my financial security with the sale of a considerable amount of our company stock as it approached its all-time high.

My retirement party, March 2007

2008 TO PRESENT

In the fall of 2008, Heidi (Shelley) moved from Colorado to the Seattle area as a single mom raising three boys because of the need to find a job in a better market. Although not Sandy's biological daughter, during her second marriage, Sandy had raised Heidi from the time she was about three years old so Sandy always considered Heidi her daughter.

Heidi's ex was a heavy drinker and made life tough on her by trying to keep her in a "one down" position. Even though the divorce decree requires him to pay monthly child support, he has not done so. Consequently, Heidi has had to weather the storm herself. She has done an excellent job as mother, father, and care giver. Although she has received considerable financial support from Sandy and me, as I write this, she has landed on her feet by securing a good position as a graphic designer, which is her chosen field.

Heidi with sons, Wyatt, Morgan, and Tanner

Heidi's ex is a real loser. When Heidi moved to Seattle, Wyatt, the oldest boy, exhibited considerable resentment because of the move. As he matures, he will no doubt come to realize what a wonderful job his mother has done and will likely see his father for what he is. His brothers, Morgan and Tanner will no doubt follow suit.

"Truth wins!"

On February 19, 2009, my brother Dan, who had been broke and in poor health for many years, died. What a blessing; he lived most of his last years in misery. I had inherited two family plots in Calvary Cemetery near Tacoma adjacent to the remains of Dad, Mom, and brother Gary and provided one of them for Danny's remains. We had a small graveside service that I officiated. What a truly sad life; a great example of how not to live!

Under Dan Baty's leadership, Emeritus continued to expand. New operations management was put in place with Granger Cobb, as co- CEO, coming to the company through an acquisition. For me it was gratifying to see a company that I played a small part in co-founding rise to the top of our industry. I do remember a comment by NME's former chairman and co-founder, Richard Eamer, that once you leave a company (he was referring to a person with a high rank, as was his position), the janitor has more authority than you. He was certainly right. In October, 2009, Granger Cobb, Emeritus co-CEO, was interviewed by the Wall Street Journal. The first question he was asked was, "Would you start by giving us a brief history of the company?" His response, "We were founded back in 1993 and went public in 1995. We were founded by Dan Baty and Ray Brandstrom, and "one other gentleman" (of course, referring to me). Well, at least I was referred to as a "gentleman" and not "the janitor". At any rate, the company seems to be doing well; I have had some brief interactions with Granger and his management team, and believe that the company has the best people in the industry.

After my retirement, the economy started to falter. Even with that, largely because of timing and luck, I was well-insulated from any negative impact from the economy. I don't need to repeat what we all experienced during those years except that I consider myself fortunate to have landed on my feet for the final countdown, whenever and however that occurs. Meanwhile, first and foremost, I have a wonderful wife and two successful children who are well on their way to a productive and happy life; I have rekindled my childhood interest in the accordion by purchasing a new one and taking lessons; I am on the boards of Murphy's Landing Marina and the recently opened Harbor History Museum (and have recently been elected President of both); we've purchased a larger yacht and cruised most of the summer of 2009 in Canada; we have two beautiful dogs (Jasmine and Jodi); and I am truly "living the dream", as son, Brian, often jousts.

Our dream yacht, "Sayonara", 2008 to present day

Jasmine and Jodi, our Labradoodle sisters

Today, a big challenge for me is my health. I have had some close calls and, so far, have survived them, but I have some chronic issues that, although, don't appear to be life-threatening, will need to be managed. Dad had a favorite placard with the saying, "Everything I like is immoral, illegal or fattening." Certainly, the last applies to me. I absolutely love good food and wine and consider it a prime joy in life.

"Staples" for my well-being

I am watching my children grow professionally and personally. That's my joy. As of this moment, daughter Tina has been married for five years and we are blessed with granddaughter, Riley. Son, Brian has become engaged to a beautiful woman, Adell Pearsall, and expects to marry next spring.

In the "Road Less Travelled", M. Scott Peck begins with the statement, "Life is difficult". My story is no exception. I believe my success lies in a combination of living day to day, having a few good friends, caring about others, having fun, paying attention to what is important to me and weathering the hard times, sometimes gracefully and sometimes not. Simply put, it's been a journey continuing to learn who I am.

"So, in a nutshell, I can say without reservation, it's been great!"

Yours with love,

Dad

October 2010

EPILOGUE

FRANK A. RUFFO JR.

November, 2010, saw one of the greatest election landslides in American history. This landslide once again renewed my faith in our system of governance as established by our founding fathers. The far left agenda of President Obama and Congress was soundly defeated, hopefully never to reappear in my life or of my children or grandchildren. Unfortunately, my State once again showed its lack of judgment by largely re-electing the same people for Congress who helped create the problem in the first place. I've concluded the voting majority in this State are urbanites who are either on the government dole, are totally altruistic, or are just plain stupid. At any rate, for the short term, politically, I've written off Washington State and, if I were you, my children, at the national level, unless you develop the ability to have a significant political impact, I would focus my attention on more productive things and rely on the American heartland to keep us on the correct political path of individual freedom. As for local politics, do what make sense for you.

The regulatory climate continues to raise havoc with business and, ultimately the jobs picture and the taxpayer. Specifically, the environmental movement is totally out of control. My hope is that during the next few years, both the federal and state government will be scaled back so that individuals will once again have a chance for reasonable self-governance. Today, many of our federal and state agencies are our God rather than our servant. We either do what they say without any real evidence to support their dictums or too bad.

"Bureaucracy at its worst!"

The religious movement speaks for itself and I've said plenty in Letter # 1 about it. In a nutshell, religious beliefs cannot be proven; they are all opinion. That said, remember to think for yourselves and have faith where it makes sense for your heart and mind.

For me, family and close friends have been my life's staple. I would not survive without this. My wonderful wife, Sandy is the rock of my life, and although we've experienced some difficult times in the remote past, she is the absolute love of my life and I have come to cherish every moment with her. I hope you find the same thing with your partner as you walk through life together. There is nothing more important!

As you now know, life is filled with ups and downs, joy and sadness, laughter and anger. Although in some instances it was difficult for me, try to keep "hate" at bay; it will destroy you if it is held on too long.

So there you have it. My hope is that this little book will provide you with a reminder of your father's life; his accomplishments as well as his mistakes. I've shared some events that don't make me proud, but I trust it shows my human vulnerability. On the plus side, I've also shared some of my glory. So please keep this so you can pass it on to your children. It has been a brief summary of my life and I have greatly enjoyed telling it.

PEARLS AND PREDICTIONS

In the body of **Letters to My Children**, my hope was to share many of the experiences, insights, theories, and lessons I learned. This section shares some of my "pearls" and also my "predictions". Because I have included them does not mean I was or am always able to follow them or that, as "pearls" or "predictions", they will ultimately prevail. No moral or prejudicial judgments are intended; as "pearls", only statements of my beliefs; as "predictions", on what I believe will likely occur.

PEARLS

- Historically, the most barbaric religion was Christianity; today it is Islam.

- "Creationism" and "evolution" are not contradictory.

- It's better to be wrong than vague.

- Today, "racism" is an over-used term to the detriment of minority groups.

- Tattoos and body decorations are on the increase because of a strong desire among many to be recognized as part of a group. Nevertheless, tattoos and much body decoration still carry with them the stigmas of criminality, counter culture or low self-esteem. If your goal is professional success:

  - Never be tattooed anywhere on your body, period. One's life will likely change course many times and tattoos are difficult and painful to remove. They will be noticed since virtually all of us will wear gym shorts or bathing suits or take a shower in a club setting from time to time. Besides, have you ever seen what "old" tattoos look like?

  - Men: avoid necklaces, earrings, bracelets, or any other jewelry that "feminizes". Be reasonable with hair and beard styles.

- Both men and women— avoid the "granola look", foot rings or leg bracelets. Avoid body piercing jewelry of any type. (Women: conservative ear piercing accepted).
- Once retired or independently wealthy (as are many professional athletes), do your own thing, but think through the impact on your total life.

- Contrary to conventional wisdom, religion and politics are great topics for discussion, particularly with those of diverse opinion. Caveat: discuss with open-minded people who will not be offended; only to share, not to convert.
- The most fascinating subjects are politics, philosophy and cosmology.
- Since it was intended that members of Congress be part time, because of what the job has become, all politicians risk damaging our country. Vote for politicians who will do the least damage.
- In the mid-1980s, Peter Lasenby, who owned Telegraph Harbor Marina, on Thetis Island in the Canadian Gulf Islands profoundly stated, "You don't need money to be happy, but it's very inconvenient if you don't have it?" I agree.
- Good health brings more wealth than money.
- Socialism is bad for our country; anyone who holds that political persuasion, should not be voted into any political office.
- Commitment and trust are the two most important ingredients in a successful marriage.
- There will always be stumbling blocks in one's life; the only thing that matters is how they are handled.

- Love conquers all only if combined with commitment, trust, hard work, and forgiveness.

- A positive attitude doesn't necessarily solve all problems, but a negative attitude will never solve anything.

- Don't ever do hard drugs or smoke tobacco!

- The universe is vast and very old. Biblical accounts are mere myth.

- Whether the earth or universe is anthropic (created specifically for humans) is doubtful but cannot be answered with certainty.

- Religions are man-made. The existence of God or afterlife are separate issues from religion.

- Three to five percent of mankind makes a significant contribution to society. It is of utmost importance to be in that group.

PREDICTIONS

- The opposite of "homosexual" is "heterosexual"; the opposite of "straight" is "crooked", not "gay". The so-called "gay pride movement" is a marketing ploy; gays will ultimately legally prevail and win marriage rights.

- The media will always be biased to the left.

- Minority groups will almost totally assimilate into our capitalistic society by the end of the century. A higher percentage of blacks will not. My reasoning—too many blacks are hung up on their "slavery" past; irrespective of equal opportunity, many will not escape the "ghetto" mentality and feel society "owes" them.

- Our government will continue to grow because of a politician's desire to continually expand laws and programs.

- There will always be a culture war in the United States between liberals and conservatives and the balance will continually shift from right of center to left of center.

- The United States will be the dominant world power for the foreseeable future.

- Entitlement programs are bankrupting our children and grandchildren. Irrespective of that, they will continue in some capacity.

- Our country (and the industrialized world) will continue to "feminize". Although some of this has been positive, the future will turn negative.

- The environmental movement has become a big power grab and has less to do about sound science and conservation and more to do about politics and control. It will become worse over time, unnecessarily further limiting freedom and private property rights.

- Conspiracy theories will always exist: i.e. the Kennedy assassination; the Council on Foreign Relations, the North American Union; the 9/11 World Trade Center Disaster. Most have (or will have) little or no merit.

- The Middle East will always be in chaos.

- Organized religion will continue to lose members.

- There will always be a chasm between the wealthy and the poor, irrespective of government philosophy.

- Human beings will become extinct, no matter what mankind does to try to prevent it. Timing is uncertain.

- Existing energy resources will dwindle and reasonable alternative sources will be slow to come because of cost, inefficiency of product, and environmentalism.

MY BEST FRIENDS

It's been said that a lucky person will have five good friends in his life. I am very lucky. I have more, along with one relative who is a close friend. It is interesting that I do not often see five out of the seven who are alive, but when we get together, it is as if there has been no time separation. More interestingly, some do not know each other or only vaguely know who they are (or were). Here they are:

Joe Carbone

Joe Gonyea

Mike Hosterman

Carl Knecht

Gary Lange (deceased)

Duncan McMillan

Mike O'Brien (deceased)

Gene Pentimonti

Ed Rogel

Joe Carbone with me

Joe Gonyea with Mike O'Brien (shortly before his death)

Me with Carl Knecht and Mike Hosterman

Me with Gary Lange (died December 26, 2005)

Duncan McMillan with me

Mike O'Brien with me (died October 4, 2010)

Gene Pentimonti and me with our wives, Jean and Sandy

Ed Rogel with me

MY CHALLENGES
AND FRUSTRATIONS

FRANK A. RUFFO JR.

- Opening medications. Most manufacturers of pharmaceuticals use packaging on bottles and individual pill packets that are nearly impossible to open unless one has a knife. Presumably they do this for safety reasons. I hate opening these.

- Packaged goods. Same thing. Impossible to open with bare hands (Radio Shack packaging is an exception—thank you!) and I've occasionally injured myself while opening them, usually cutting myself with my knife.

- I park in the "outfield" in parking lots as far away from other cars as possible. Invariably, someone will park right next to me.

- Two people (usually two women) carrying on a continuous conversation in close proximity to me while I'm on an exercise machine at a gym.

- Driving behind exceedingly slow drivers, particularly through my hometown city of Gig Harbor and in the left hand lanes of a freeway.

- Waiting in line. A real pain in the rear.

- Disagreements with Sandy.

- Repair jobs/projects that do not go smoothly.

- Nonproductive people with sound minds and bodies who have the government/taxpayer support them.

- Far left liberals who support big government and entitlement programs in exact opposition to what our founders intended.

- The religious right who believe their way is the only way.

- Illegal immigrants.

- The gay rights movement.

- Computers that don't work the way they were designed to work.

- Plane travel of more than three hours, particularly when seated in an area occupied by ill-mannered or crying infants and toddlers.

PHOTO GALLERY

Papa Ruffo's 82nd birthday (his last), he died November 5, 1955

Uncle Rick (Ruffo) and Aunt Mabel (me in the back), 1955

Me, Gary, Danny, 1959-61

Dad and Mom, Papa Gus (Carbone) and Nana Helen, Gary, Danny, and Sassy

Me with family prior to leaving for Santa Clara, fall 1960

Two Santa Claran's, Joe Gonyea and me, 1961

*Me and roommate, Jack Brady; our houseboat home, Seattle, 1963
(Jack was killed in Vietnam, April 3, 1968)*

LETTERS TO MY CHILDREN

New Ensign/Lt. Ames/ Chief Denny, Kilo Company, May 1965

"On duty" (mother ship, USS Pluck, in background), 1966

FRANK A. RUFFO JR.

My crew and me on the USS Pluck, May 1966

My second tour, USS Bennington (CVS 20), Nov. 1966-May, 1968

LETTERS TO MY CHILDREN

Aboard "Big Ben", Yokosuka, Japan, Feb. 67

*Mom with me, Joanne, Brian and Ginger,
Everett, WA, backyard, 1973*

Brian, Salashan, Oregon., 1975

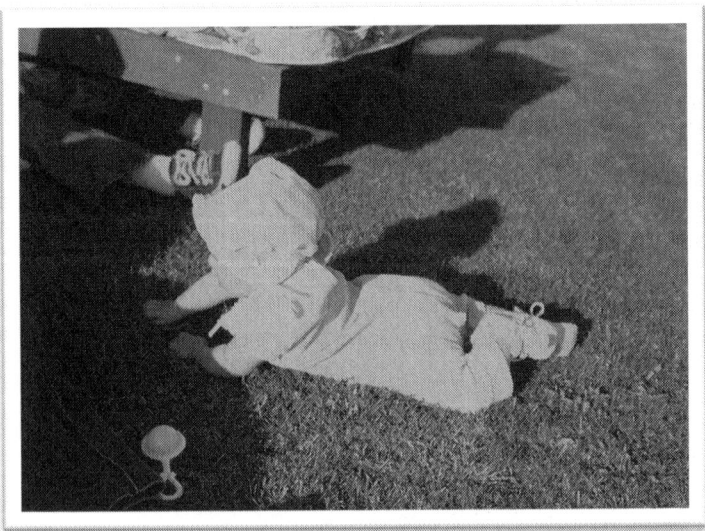

Tina, summer 1977

LETTERS TO MY CHILDREN

Tina and Brian, Edgewood home back yard, 1981

Tina and Nana Mary, Edgewood home deck, 1981

Dad and Mom, Arizona, 1988

Brian and future daughter-in-law Adell, Hawaii 2010

Son-in-law Erik Knutson and daughter Tina, 2010

Granddaughter Riley Knutson, December 2010

Sandy and me, 1985

Sandy and me, 1998

Sandy and me at Tina's wedding, 2005

Sandy and me, Roche Harbor, 2009

FRANK A. RUFFO JR.

ACKNOWLEDGEMENTS

For the last several years, I toyed with the idea of writing my life story. Not because I have done anything famous or all that unusual, but rather, I believe my story shows that flexibility and taking advantage of opportunity raises the chance of achieving happiness. More importantly, I wanted to memorialize it for those close to me.

When I retired in July 2007, I began to seriously consider the endeavor. When I discussed the project with my wife, Sandy, she was very supportive. I found the thought of the task daunting, but decided I would someday plunge into it.

When I finished my last draft in the fall of 2010, I finally felt I had completed the basic project, but knew nothing about editing, publishing or printing. Erik Knutson, my son-in law, worked on the initial format. Then, "my other daughter", Heidi Shelley, whose talents lie in graphic design, graciously agreed to take over completion of the book. Heidi spent many hours recommending language changes, formatting, designing, and coordinating the final printing of the book. Lastly, my wife, Sandy, spent hours proof reading the final draft and corrected many flaws.

For each of their contributions, they have my heartfelt thanks.

Frank Ruffo

January, 2011

BIBLIOGRAPHY

Author	Title	Publisher	Year
Armstrong, Karen	A History of God	Random House	1993
Arthur, John	Morality and Moral Controversies	Prentice Hall	2005
Avlon, John	Wingnuts	Beast Books	2010
Barcalow, Emmett	Open Questions	Wadsworth Publishing	1993
Beck, Glen	An Inconvenient Book	Simon and Schuster	2007
Black, Earl & Merle	Divided America	Simon and Schuster	2007
Blackburn, Simon	Truth	Oxford University Press	2005
Dawkins, Richard	The God Delusion	Bantam Press	2008
Flynn, Daniel J.	Intellectual Morons	Crown Publishing	2004
Friedman, George	The Next 100 Years	Random House	2009
Gingrich, Newt	Real Change	Regnery Publishing	2009
Gore, Al	An Inconvenient Truth	Penguin Group	2006
Harris, Sam	Letter to a Christian Nation	Random House	2006
Hitchens, Christopher	The Portable Atheist	De Capo Press	2007
Impey, Chris	How It Ends	WW Norton	2010
Krishnamurti, J.	Think on These Things	Harper and Row	1970
Krugman, Paul	The Conscience of a Liberal	WW Norton	2007
Kupelian, David	How Evil Works	Simon and Schuster	2010
Miller, Kenneth	Finding Darwin's God	Harper Collins	1999
O'Reilly, Bill	Pinheads and Patriots	Harper Collins	2010
Paine, Thomas	The Age of Reason	Barnes and Noble	2006 *
Paine, Thomas	The Crisis	Prometheus Books	2008 *
Paine, Thomas	Rights of Man	Barnes and Noble	2004 *
Peck, M. Scott	The Road Less Traveled	Simon and Schuster	1978
Peterson, Peter G.	Running on Empty	Farrar, Straus & Giroux	2004
Redman, Ben	The Portable Voltaire	Viking Penguin, Inc.	1977
Sagan, Carl	The Varieties of Scientific Experience	Penguin Books	2006
Smith, Adam	Wealth of Nations	Barnes and Noble	2004 *
Thomson, Keith	Before Darwin	Harper Collins	2005
Weisman, Alan	The World Without Us	St. Martin's Press	2007
Wills, Gary	Under God	Simon and Schuster	1990
Woods, Len	Handbook of World Religions	Barbour Publishing	2008
	The Holy Bible	Catholic Books	1958
	The Way, the Living Bible	Tyndall House	1976
	The World Almanac	World Almanac Books	2010

*ORIGINAL PUBLICATION DATES:

Age of Reason	1794-95
The Crisis	1918
Rights of Man	1894
Wealth of Nations	1776

Made in the USA
Charleston, SC
23 March 2011